JAMES HOGG

A

NEW ASSESSMENTS

JAMES HOGG

DOUGLAS GIFFORD

THE RAMSAY HEAD PRESS EDINBURGH

First published in 1976 by
The Ramsay Head Press
36 North Castle Street
Edinburgh EH2 3BN

With the support of the
Scottish Arts Council

Printed in Great Britain by
Macdonald Printers (Edinburgh) Limited
Edgefield Road, Loanhead, Midlothian

Contents

In memory of
Keith Wright
friend and colleague

INTRODUCTION

A LITERARY re-assessment of the creative achievement of James Hogg is long overdue. For too long he has been known as the simple shepherd poet of Ettrick, with a poetry ranked below that of Burns, Fergusson and Ramsay, and hardly read—let alone taught—as a significant part of the Scottish literary tradition. Even the recent and deserved attention given to his *The Private Memoirs and Confessions of a Justified Sinner* has tended to overshadow his other major work, such as his epic and comic Border romance, *The Three Perils of Man,* his shorter anti-romantic novels like *Basil Lee* and *An Edinburgh Bailie* and his many superb, starkly told short stories. This study argues that Hogg's poetry can be seen as a preliminary stage in the development of his real genius, which, owing to the nature of his Border roots and background, was for the retelling of folk tales, especially those of the Border, be they supernatural, comic or grotesque. Sometimes, as in *The Brownie of Bodsbeck,* or *The Three Perils of Man,* these tales are presented as though they are a kind of historical romance, or, as in *The Justified Sinner,* as religious satire—but beneath these guises lies always Hogg's living awareness of an oral tradition going back to and beyond the Border legends and Ballads. His unique genius lies in his ability to recreate the atmosphere of mystery, the vividness and immediacy of detail, the comic richness and the grotesquerie of his traditional material, and to evoke as not even Scott or Stevenson could the sense of another haunting world next to our own. Thus the emphasis in this short study is on Hogg's fiction, although his poetry and prose is

7

also considered. Similarly the biographical discussion has been limited to the baldest outline of his life, and even then only where related to the main issue of his creative achievement and the consideration of whether he ranks as a major writer of fiction within the Scottish and English literary traditions.

Basic to the entire study is the idea of dualism within Hogg's life and work; the first giving rise to the second. There is the Ettrick Hogg and there is the Edinburgh Hogg. Both were necessary to create *The Justified Sinner,* but paradoxically the crisis of identity and confidence which they generated—a familiar story with Ramsay, Fergusson and Burns before him—goes a long way to explaining many of Hogg's complete failures, like *The Three Perils of Women.* We also gain a telling insight into the culturally destructive snobbery and distortion of literary values which increasingly dominated Edinburgh and Scottish Literature throughout the nineteenth century.

Chapter One

ETTRICK HOGG AND
EDINBURGH HOGG

Hogg's life splits clearly into two periods separated by the year 1810.[1] He was born about 1770[2] in the parish of Ettrick, among the highest, bleakest and loneliest hills of the Scottish Borders. His father was "a hard working shepherd, a well-meaning, well-living man," an enthusiastic reader of the Bible; his mother a shrewd, independent woman who was famed for her huge knowledge of Border Ballads and legends. They were too poor to let Hogg have much schooling, and after less than a year's sporadic local education, Hogg left his formal education with a love of Bible reading but little ability to write. Thereafter, till 1791, he worked at odd jobs with horses, cows and sheep with many different masters, and read Blind Harry, Ramsay's *Gentle Shepherd* and theological writings like Harvey's *Meditations among the Tombs* and Burnet's [*Sacred*] *Theory of the Earth*.

In 1791 he went to work with the Laidlaws of Blackhouse. Finding a friend for life in William Laidlaw, congenial work as shepherd, and a library, he stayed there ten years; and during this time began to put the songs he had made up for his fellow workers on paper, decided to emulate Burns, joined (like Ramsay, Fergusson and Burns before him) a literary society, made up of fellow-shepherds, to improve himself; and published *Scottish Pastorals, Poems, Songs, &c.* in 1801, a rushed, premature collection of poems much influenced by Ramsay. About this time he also met Walter Scott as the latter was collecting for his

Minstrelsy of the Scottish Border, gaining (apart from one major quarrel) another friend for life.

From 1801 to 1804 Hogg made annual trips to the Highlands and Islands, the last being with a view towards arranging emigration to Harris—but with the bad financial luck that haunted him all his life he lost the savings necessary for the farm he was due to take there. For the next three years he worked in Cumberland and Nithsdale in some poverty. Yet all this time his fame as a shepherd poet was growing. At Nithsdale Allan Cunningham had gone to some trouble to find him and recite his poems to him. The *Scots Magazine* had been printing his ballads and songs regularly since 1803, and in 1807 *The Mountain Bard,* a collection from these and other ballad imitations appeared successfully, along with his prize-winning *The Shepherd's Guide,* a treatise on sheep diseases. From the rewards of his poetic and practical ventures he leased two farms. The difficulties of running both, Hogg and his partner's lively social habits ("feasting, drinking, dancing, and fiddling, etc.," according to a visitor at the time) put the sheep on the wrong side of the hill and the farms in the hands of creditors. Whether through distrust of "Jamie the Poeter" as poet, or simply as failed farmer, no one now wanted Hogg as shepherd in Yarrow. In 1810 in desperation, at forty years old, he went to Edinburgh to be "a literary man."

It is useful to stop and consider 1810 as a pivot year in Hogg's life, separating Ettrick from Edinburgh. Of course the Border and capital experiences mingle, just as in his work the Ballad inspirations and the aspirations to conventional and current kinds of poetry and fiction are mixed. But since his work is so marked on the one hand by the distinction between what he inherited from his Border background, giving an authenticity of vision which is true to his basic nature, and on the other his perpetually shifting, ever-imitative desire to find a "vision" and form acceptable to a polite Edinburgh and British audience, I feel one should consider these two sides separately.

The Ettrick Hogg may have lacked formal education, but he grew up with his imagination richly nourished by vital and vivid Ballads, legends, Bible stories and chapbooks, until he naturally came in contact with the other and formal literary traditions of Scotland. His mother had an abundance of Ballad lore, as Scott discovered, and made her house a meeting place and a part of the chain of oral tradition. She was aware of the tradition too, as separate from the literary, and she sharply criticised Scott for "freezing" in print what should have been left as an organic process. Ballads like "Auld Maitland," she said

> were made for singin' an' no for readin', but ye hae broken the charm noo, an' they'll never be sung mair.[3]

The influence of the Ballads on Hogg's poetry can be seen at a glance in *The Mountain Bard* or *The Queen's Wake;* but it cannot be stressed enough how much this Ballad background is the basis of both content and form in the bulk and the best of his fiction.

A Ballad is a folksong that tells a story with stress on the crucial situation, tells it by letting the action unfold itself in event and speech, and tells it objectively with little comment or intrusion of personal bias.

Action centred on a single situation, which may be

either the culminating point in a larger series of events or an isolated happening of sensational value is the first constant discoverable in the Ballads.[4]

Such descriptions fit Hogg's terse, laconic short stories completely. One is always aware in Hogg's stories of dream, apparition, or mystery that the vivid incident is his imaginative "unit." Even in the longer, more ambitious works such as *The Three Perils of Man* one is aware of Hogg's awkwardness with prolonged structural control, and his relief in finding himself telling a story, in the traditional manner, within the story. Frequently he drops intermediate narrative between speeches, letting the vernacular speeches or dramatic monologues themselves carry the story. And Hogg was even accused of bad taste when in fact he was working with *another* ballad tradition, that of the "impersonal attitude to the events of the story," which in Hogg's work often manifests itself as a curious unconventional treatment of sympathetic and favoured characters in his narrative. With the "swordstroke" suddenness of the ballads such protagonists can suffer death and removal from the story right in the middle of events—or just at a point where with the "conventional" treatment they would be regarded as vitally involved in the development or denouement of the plot. It was only at Scott's desire that Hogg altered the death by burning of the "hero" of "The Witch of Fife." Similarly he caused the early destruction of the only hero to be found in *The Justified Sinner,* George Dalcastle, and, outstandingly, of one of the most likeable comic figures in his *The Three Perils of Man,* the shrewd old fisherman Sandy Yellowlees. It is almost as though Scott were suddenly to kill off Bailie Nicol Jarvie early in *Rob Roy*—but in Hogg's novel the

12

impersonal and Balladic swiftness of fate here and in the hanging of the yeoman Heaton serves to make a superb ironic comment on what chivalrous wars mean to peasants.

Indeed throughout Hogg's tales there is an understatement of tragic events and sentiment which is older even than the Ballads, going back to the sagas.

> I knew a man well, whose name was Andrew Murray, that perished in the snow on Minchmoor; and he had taken it so deliberately, that he had buttoned his coat, and folded his plaid, which he had laid beneath his head for a bolster.[5]

And throughout Hogg's poetry and fiction, from "Kilmeny" to *The Three Perils of Man,* is another ballad characteristic—that of timelessness of setting, vagueness of territorial reference, and even vaguer temporal detail. Read the the opening of "Ewan McGabhar," with its oral style, its reference to wars in times unspecified involving queens unnamed and kingdoms and countries of mystery. This is the world of "Sir Patrick Spens" and Ballad openings like "It fell aboot the Lammas Tide. . . ." Actors like Lord Downan and Colin More appear in the story as suddenly and with as little background location in time or in terms of the story itself as, say, Inverey in "The Baron o' Brackley." Even in historically "placed" tales like *The Brownie of Bodsbeck* or *The Justified Sinner* Hogg manages to introduce the timeless Ballad atmosphere with devices like Nannie's songs in the first ("But in yon houm there is a kirk/. .. An' in that pew there sat a king/Wha signed the deed we maun ever rue" or "He wasna King o' fair Scotland/Though King o' Scotland he should hae been . . .") and Penpunt's Auchtermuchty stories in the second.

But most of all Hogg draws on that aspect of the Ballads which Gregory Smith referred to as "the horns of Elfland,"[6] the "other world" of Thomas the Rhymer and Tam Lin. Some short stories like "Mary Burnet," "The Brownie of the Black Haggs" and "The Mysterious Bride" are virtually Ballads of this type turned into prose tales. Like, say, "The Daemon Lover," they present a stylised and patterned picture of an offender who awakens the wrath of a mysterious, pagan and yet Christian power which sends its representative to destroy the unnatural disturber of simple community harmony. Hogg, like the Ballads, presents his tale with all the traditional hints and clues to the identity of the strange visitor and the supernatural nature of the occurrence. Where "The Daemon Lover" has a strange ship, stranger mariners and the girl realises through these clues that the journey is to hell, Hogg similarly uses colours (green and gold signify fairy powers) and figures like the traditional "wee, wee man" and diabolic metaphor to imply his supernatural meaning. Here is the same love of "seven long years," of "a league but barely"; and when one has read these tales it is easier to grasp the true provenance of *The Justified Sinner,* and to realise that it too has its connection with the Ballads. Is it not similar in its method, with its red-letter hints as to the devilish identity of the mysterious Gilmartin, and its judgement of the sinner, to the method and progress of "The Daemon Lover"?

Sometimes, as in *The Three Perils of Man, The Hunt of Eildon,* or "Mary Burnet," Hogg's other world is that of the Ballad *Tam Lin* or of True Thomas the Rhymer of Ercildoune. Sometimes as in *The Justified Sinner* or "The Brownie of the Black Haggs" or "The Cameronian Preacher's Tale" the other world is a bleaker place dominated by a harshly just and

Christian Providence. Often the forces of the other world are eventually shown to be illusory, extended deceptions, as in *The Brownie of Bodsbeck,* or "A Tale of Good Queen Bess." Hogg even uses his imagination independently of tradition to create a fantastic landscape such as that of "Kilmeny" or *The Pilgrims of the Sun,* where the land to which the pure girl goes is one of ideal beauty and light, or as in the arctic escapades of Allan Gordon and his polar bear companion; and "other world" forces are used for sheer fun in "May of the Moril Glen" and "The Witch of Fife." More analysis of the influence of Ballad background on major stories will follow, but it is of crucial importance to understand how much he owes to it, and to the oral tales in prose which his mother also knew so well.

> Our mother's mind was well fortified by a good system of Christian religion . . . yet her mind was stored with tales of spectres, ghosts, fairies, brownies . . . which had an influence on James's mind altogether unperceived at the time. . . . He was remarkably fond of . . . tales of kings, giants, knights, fairies, kelpies, brownies, etc.[7]

Edith Batho has traced one poem of Hogg's to a very ancient past.[8] In like fashion, could these tales, different from Ballads, not be part of that common heritage which produced medieval romances like *King Horn, Havelok the Dane, Gawayne and the Green Knight* and *Sir Orfeo*? From this background Hogg gained his sense of Good and Bad as profoundly real, concrete forces, his sense of animal nature, human nature and "the other world" being an organic whole, his "reductive idiom" which so often mocks the courtly tradition of chivalry and juxtaposes it with an earthy realism devoid of false sentiment. The world of *Sir Orfeo is* related to the world of *The Hunt of Eildon,* and "Ewan McGabhar" bears striking resemblance to *King Horn* or *Havelok.* In many ways the creators of all these had more in common than Hogg had with John Wilson or John Gibson Lockhart, the Edinburgh culture of his day or British Romantic poetry.

But without going so far back Hogg could select endless tales from local, shepherd superstitions and legends, as he tells us he did in his *Winter Evening Tales* of 1820. He frequently refers to himself as merely an editor of material current in the Borders. Indeed he could draw from family tradition for much of it. They had witches amongst their forebears; Hogg's own wraith had been seen when he was close to death in childhood, and his grandfather Will o' Phaup

> was the last man of this wild region, who heard, saw, and conversed with the fairies; and that not once . . . but at sundry times and seasons.[9]

His Uncle John Hoy had attended sacraments on the moors with the Covenanters, sending his dog off on her own to collect the sheep, and another uncle, supposed rich in Ballads, gave Hogg instead

> a deluge . . . of errors, sins, lusts, covenants broken, burned and buried. . . .[10]

Fairy lore and family tales of fiery religious zeal are two of the strongest elements in all Hogg's later poems and stories. From his earliest work he falls into a habit of presenting himself merely as editor of material current in his Border community. In the very early *Spy* magazine tale "The Wife of Lochmaben" his attitude is established. The murder therein happened "not many years ago" and was told to Hogg "by a strolling gypsy of the town . . . pretty nearly as follows." Even *The Justified Sinner* will be presented from this stance. Indeed, in all Hogg's fiction remarkably little is *not* fed by this basic Border and oral stream, be it supernatural or religious, married with his later reading of writers like Anne Grant, Dougal Graham, Wodrow and the like[11] He tells us in *The Brownie of Bodsbeck* that

> The general part is taken from Wodrow, and the local part from the relation of my own father, who had the best possible traditionary account of the incidents.[12]

Now this basis of Hogg's fiction may not have been historically accurate, and indeed caused Scott's violent dislike of a novel on the topic of Claverhouse and the Covenanters which took such a radically opposed view of both sides from *Old Mortality,* turning Clavers into a butchering sadist, a cold-hearted anticipation of Gilmartin in *The Justified Sinner,* but it cannot be denied that it gave Hogg a vivid, living source material:

> Clavers exerted himself that day in such a manner, galloping over precipices, and cheering on his dragoons, that all the country people who beheld him believed him to be a devil, or at least mounted on one. The marks of that infernal courser's feet are shown to this day on a steep hill nearly perpendicular, below the Bubbly Craig. . . .[13]

> Clavers actually traversed the country more like an exterminating angel, than the commander of a civilised army.[14]

To Scott's accusation that it was an "unfair picture of the times and the existing characters altogether" Hogg, unmoved, and sure of his ground, said

I dinna ken, Mr Scott. It is the picture I have been brought up in the belief o' sin' ever I was born, and I had it frae them whom I was most bound to honour and believe—

—and alleging the atrocities to be true, continued

and that's a great deal mair than you can say for your tale "Auld Mortality."[15]

Would for Hogg's art that such confidence had stayed with him! But later, when Scott was to accuse him of writing merely "by random," and "without once considering what you are going to write about," Hogg agreed, but had a vital point to make in addition.

When my tale is traditionary, the work is easy, as I then see my way before me, though the tradition be ever so short, but in all my prose works of imagination, knowing little of the world, I sail on without star or compass.[16]

We have to read this carefully—for Hogg is saying a wrong thing as well as a right. Wrongly he accepts adverse opinion of work he *had* at the time of its creation valued highly, like *The Justified Sinner* or *The Three Perils of Man,* which are most certainly highly imaginative, and also come from tradition. But very rightly he stresses how crucial an element his Border background is to his creative imagination. Two early stories, both presented through a peasant boy hero close to Hogg himself, illustrate this. In the first, "Duncan Campbell," Duncan

would have been completely happy, if it had not been for the fear of spirits. When the conversation chanced to turn on the Piper o' Dewar, the Maid of Polar or the Pedlar o' Thirlestane Mill, often have we lain with the bedclothes drawn over our heads till nearly suffocated. We loved the fairies and the brownies, and even felt a little partiality for the mermaids, on account of their beauty and charming songs; but we were a little jealous of the water kelpies, and always kept aloof from the frightsome pools. We hated the devil most heartily, though we were not much afraid of him; but a ghost! oh, dreadful! [17]

And Barnaby the shepherd boy of "The Woolgatherer" tells us that

The deil an' his adgents, they fash nane but the good fock; the Cameronians, an' the praying ministers . . . the bogles . . . meddle wi' nane but the guilty; the murderer and the mansworn . . . the fairies, they're very harmless . . . but if fock neglect kirk ordinances, they see after *them*. Then the brownie, he's a kind of half-spirit half-man. . . .[18]

Apart from establishing "rules" that help us understand the progress of many short stories and the entire development of *The Justified Sinner,* these quotations demonstrate both how Hogg's Christian and pagan worlds are, as it were, opposite ends of a spectrum, and how deep in his bones this lore must have been.

Two important, if slightly digressive, questions occur naturally here. Did Hogg believe in the supernatural for a part or all of his life? How religious a man was he?

The answer to the first can never be authoritative, but we can assume that as a child and adolescent he was like Duncan or Barnaby. Thereafter the evidence of the notes to *The Mountain Bard,* the continued use of the supernatural as a staple in nearly all his stories till he died suggests that he never lost a certain simple faith that the strange events which he represents in his tales had actually happened in a way which defied rational solution. Consider as late an article as "Nature's Magic Lantern," published in 1837, where events which have occurred all over Scotland reminiscent of the horrific scenes at Arthur's Seat in *The Justified Sinner,* are set down as inexplicable.[19] But against this must be set Hogg's increasing practice, after and including *The Brownie of Bodsbeck* (1818), of following the "Tam o' Shanter" "either/or" statement of supernatural/rational ambiguity, a practice seen at its most subtle and deliberately inconclusive in *The Justified Sinner,* "The Brownie of the Black Haggs" and "The Baron St. Gio." I will say more about this crucial, *intentional* creation of dual, mutually exclusive interpretations when dealing with *The Justified Sinner,* but it does suggest that Hogg's "solution" to the dilemma of reconciling Border belief with later-developed and "Edinburgh" rationalism was in fact a clever sleight of hand evasion of the issue by allowing both belief and scepticism to exist together, leaving the reader to choose between them. I certainly do not think that the following statement of 1830, only a few years before death, can be taken at simple face value.

A great number of people now-a-days are beginning broadly to insinuate that there are no such things as ghosts, or spiritual beings visible to mortal man. Even Sir Walter Scott is turned renegade, and, with his stories made up of half and, like Nathaniel Gow's toddy, is trying to throw cold water on the most certain, though the most impalpable, phenomena of human nature. The bodies are daft. Heaven mend their wits! . . . I wish they had been where I have often been. . . .[20]

Considering that Hogg himself had mastered the "half-and-half" technique to perfection at the same time as Scott in, say, "Wandering Willie's Tale" from *Redgauntlet* (1824), and that he goes on to tell a ghost tale that happened on the road to "Balmawhapple," that comic creation of his own, one concludes that his eventual stance on the subject of the supernatural was inconclusive, at least—and sly.

To the question concerning his religious beliefs one can be more sure in answering that he shares the views of his many heroes like Wat of Chapelhope of *The Brownie of Bodsbeck,* or the Laird of Dalcastle in *The Justified Sinner;* that Hogg himself was "an honest, conscientious, good old fashioned man, but he made no great fuss about religion. . . ."[21] To this it need only be added that nevertheless his parents seem to have acted as buffers between Hogg and a Border background of devout Presbyterianism of a disruptive and evangelical kind, as exemplified in Thomas Boston, minister in Ettrick forty years before Hogg's birth, and zealous proponent of creeds which Hogg attacked in *The Justified Sinner*. Thus Hogg was steeped in Presbyterian atmosphere, argument and reading yet at the same time through family and personal inclination and later Edinburgh experience developing into a most moderate, tolerant Christian. Indeed, sometimes in his speculations about the nature of heaven and the possible reincarnatory nature of man's moral life he ran the risk of being accused of mild "heresy"—as in his long poem *The Pilgrims of the Sun,* with its "extravagant and heterodox"[22] positioning of God in the centre of the Sun, and consequent justification of sun worship. More frequently and more typically, throughout Hogg's work from Thomas Boston's dealings with the Pedlar's Ghost in *The Mountain Bard* to the comic prayers of Davie Tait with their deep peasant kindness in *The Brownie of Bodsbeck,* from the terrible curse of the Reverend Wringhim on the Laird of Dalcastle to the White Lady who appals the Justified Sinner with her severe looks, from the "hideous fiends" who gnash on him with their teeth and clench their crimson paws in his face to that strangest expression of Evil, Merodach the Brownie of the Black Haggs, we are aware of a traditional, non-Edinburgh attitude to religion and the supernatural, fostered rather than checked by its religious leaders like Boston, and if anything deepened in Hogg by close reading of works such as *The Pilgrim's Progress,* Wodrow's *Sufferings of the Church of Scotland* and Bishop Burnet's *The [Sacred] Theory of the Earth.*

All this belonged to a very different society from that of Edinburgh in 1810. Hogg was to fall victim to the ever-growing Edinburgh and Scottish upper and middle-class snobbery of the late eighteenth and nineteenth century. Ramsay, Fergusson and Burns had met this snobbery—indeed that feature common to them all, what David Daiches has called "the crisis of identity," arose directly out of the unsureness of these writers as to where their audience and their significant critics were to be found. And while there has been much discussion about the general Scottish cultural background to Hogg and his contemporaries, insufficient attention has been paid, in particular studies, to the real significance of his relationships with his friends and literary contemporaries.

Edwin Muir has asserted that no complete and healthy critical awareness existed in Edinburgh at the beginning of the nineteenth century; this was replaced by frequent and almost doctrinaire disagreements between the two great periodicals of the day, the Whig *Edinburgh Review* and the Tory *Blackwood's Magazine*. But going beyond this kind of opposition, one discovers that genteel standards of taste and politeness have had an even more serious and adverse effect on the quality of Scottish literature. Leaving Scott's unique vision aside, one discovers Susan Ferrier abandoning fiction after 1832 because of a sense of the activity being socially unacceptable. She refused, moreover, to read John Galt's fiction because she thought his vulgarity "beats print." John Gibson Lockhart's two considerable attempts at the serious investigation of the darker aspects of Scottish psychology, *Adam Blair* (1822) and *Matthew Wald* (1824), caused shock and disapproval to a degree which we now find difficult to understand, and which may have caused Lockhart to abandon fiction. The Edinburgh which admired the fiction of John Wilson ("Christopher North") was in fact bound to find Hogg's tales offensive, with their rude Border health and their directness of expression.

Into this society, like a bull into a china shop, came Hogg in 1810, with his plan to run a weekly magazine, *The Spy*. With his Border background of rich oral poetry and story, and his wholeness of attitude which integrated manual labour and poetic vision, Hogg was an anachronism in nineteenth-century Edinburgh. His directness and honesty of approach attracted patrons at first, but then embarrassed them. And a curious and distasteful element emerges from Hogg's relations with some of his patrons. They kept up the pretence of being his friend, when they were in fact exploiting him.

Scott was not one of these false friends. He did help Hogg frequently but in his capacity of social superior. Scott's letters to others about Hogg are littered with references to "the great Caledonian Boar," or the "hog's pearls" (referring to Hogg's novel *The Three Perils of Women*). One remembers Hogg's annoyance at how Scott would "control" him in public; and on one occasion Scott's help was offered on the condition that Hogg put his poetical talent under lock and key forever.[23] Scott would give money and even well-meant criticism about the lack of planning in Hogg's stories. But in terms of a full, frank interchange of ideas between literary, social and intellectual equals, Scott failed Hogg. The Scott of Hogg's *Domestic Manners of Sir Walter Scott* had "a too strong leaning to the old aristocracy"—"a prodigious devotion for titled rank, amounting almost to adoration." This Scott was bored at shepherds' discussions and "quizzed" his simple hosts in superior fashion, and supervised Hogg's table manners on public occasions. The relationship is found in a nutshell in Scott's dinner joke:

> If ye reave the Hoggs o' Fauldshope
> Ye harry Harden's gear . . .

—that is, insult Scott's vassal.[24]

And if Scott, the counsellor of writers the world over, could ignore or fail to see the real talent of Hogg, then one is not surprised to find lesser Edinburgh figures following his lead. Hogg's highly complex relations with *Blackwood's Magazine* illustrate this perfectly. To sum them up; Hogg appears genuinely to have had a major hand in starting the magazine in 1817, beginning the famous parody of biblical writing in the scandalous "Chaldee manuscript" which lampooned most of the notables of Edinburgh at the time.

His new friends, John Wilson and John Gibson Lockhart, fresh from Oxford, lacking Hogg's geniality, then re-worked this. But they allowed the new savage note which resulted to be attributed to Hogg as much as to themselves. It is ironic in the light of this and later exploitation, that in 1817 Hogg had advised William Blackwood that

> Wilson's papers have a masterly cast about them; a little custom would make him the best periodical writer of the age—keep hold of him.[25]

It seems that as Wilson and Lockhart grew more friendly with Blackwood, Hogg was increasingly viewed through glasses coloured by snobbery. Lockhart was not so bad—indeed he paid a marvellous tribute to Hogg's "unaffected simplicity . . . modesty and confidence such as well becomes a man of genius," along with his "noble consciousness of perfect independence," in his *Peter's Letters to His Kinsfolk* (1818). But is there still something here of the ritual of praising the Scottish peasant-poet, as was gone through with Burns?

There is no doubt about the attitude of John Wilson, whom one sees more and more as an embodiment of all that was unhealthy in Scottish literature of the period, with his warped genius, his double-dealing, and his sloppy sentimental verse and fiction. Here is a typically ambiguous Wilson treatment of Hogg. It combines the depiction of Hogg as buffoon with apparent affection, in a way which Wilson's "Noctes Ambrosianae," that series of imaginary gatherings involving the Ettrick shepherd, was to continue throughout the eighteen-twenties—a treatment particularly poisonous in its trading on its victim's good nature.

You, James, are the rough diamond he [the author of an article on Hogg in *The Scots Magazine*] proposes to describe with mathematical exactness. Really, I felt, during the solemn note of preparation, much as one feels in a drawing room, when, the stupid servant having forgotten to announce the name, the door slowly moves on its hinges, and some splendid stranger is expected to appear; but when, to the pleased surprise of the assembled company, in bounced you yourself, the worthy and most ingenious shepherd, rubbing your ungloved hands (would I were a glove on that hand!) as if you were washing them, with a good humoured smile on your honest face, enough to win every heart, and with a pair of top boots . . . instantly recalling the shining imagery of Day and Martin's patent blacking.[26]

Hogg wrote about this to Blackwood:

I am almost ruing the day that I ever saw you. I have had letters, newspapers, and magazines poured in upon me. . . . The country is full of impatience. No-one has any right to publish aught in my name without consulting me. . . . It is confoundedly hard that I should be made a tennis ball between contending parties. If you can find out by the writ or otherwise who the shabby scoundrel is that writes the enclosed, pray return it to him in a blank cover.[27]

Wilson could be even more direct. In 1821 he wrote:

Pray, who wishes to know anything about his life? Who indeed cares a single farthing whether he be at this blessed moment dead or alive? Only picture to yourself a stout country lout, with a bushel of hair on his shoulders that had not been raked for months, enveloped in a coarse plaid impregnated with tobacco, with a prodigious mouthful of immeasurable tusks, and a dialect that set all conjecture at defiance, lumbering in suddenly upon the elegant retirement of Mr Miller's back shop. . . . What would he [Hogg] himself have thought, if a large surly brown bear, or a huge baboon, had burst open his door when he was at breakfast. . . . ?[28]

Wilson's statement about the country lout lumbering in on elegant retirement could stand for polite Edinburgh's heart-felt attitude to Hogg. It purports to come from a friend—how much worse must his enemies have been! But it tells us more about polite Edinburgh than it does about Hogg. The truth is that Hogg was bound to clash with the Edinburgh *literati*. Of the trio who wrote the "Chaldee manuscript," only Hogg managed to stay friendly with the Whigs like Thomas Pringle who were satirised therein. Hogg, of an older generation, with no affectation or "side," was incapable of snobbery. This is charmingly revealed in the picture of one of Hogg's typical parties held in Watson's *Selkirk and Peeblesshire Inn* whenever he came up to Edinburgh from the Borders in later life. Grassmarket meal dealers, genteel and slender young men from Parliament House, printers from the Cowgate, booksellers from the New Town all rubbed shoulders.

Between a couple of young advocates sits a decent grocer from Bristo Street, and amidst a host of shop lads from the Lucken booths is perched a stiffish young probationer who scarcely knows whether he should be here or not. . . . Jolly, honest-like bakers in pepper-and-salt coats give great uneasiness to squads of black coats in juxtaposition with them;

27

and several dainty looking youths in white neck-cloths and black silk eyeglass ribbons are evidently much discomposed by a rough type of horsedealer, who has got in amongst them and keeps calling out all kinds of coarse jokes to a crony. . . . Many of Mr Hogg's Selkirkshire store farming friends are there with their well oxygenated complexions and Dandy-Dinmont-like bulk of figure. . . . If a representative assembly had been made up from all the classes of the community, it could not have been more miscellaneous than this company assembled by a man to whom, in the simplicity of his heart, all company seemed alike acceptable.[29]

All Hogg's writing reflects his two worlds. Sometimes he writes strongly and confidently as an independent Borderer, aware of the validity of his own tradition, and sometimes he tries to be a poet and novelist in the style and content of the time, almost always with disastrous results. But this study will argue that, for all his lapses of taste, his bathetic incongruities and imitations of writers of the age which reveal his deep-seated personal and creative insecurity, he did attempt to reconcile these worlds, to fuse his Border experience with his later awareness that Edinburgh and Scottish literature had strengths and disciplines necessary to his genius. Hogg could see the best in both worlds, but his tragedy lies in the fact that polite and literary Edinburgh could see the best as existing only in its own.

NOTES

1. For further study of Hogg, see Edith C. Batho, *The Ettrick Shepherd*, 1927; Alan L. Strout, *The Life and Letters of James Hogg*, vol. I, 1946 (only volume); Louis Simpson, *James Hogg, A Critical Study*, 1962; *James Hogg; Selected Poems*, ed. Douglas Mack, 1970. For some account of the background, see Edwin Muir, *Scott and Scotland*, 1936; David Craig, *Scottish Literature and the Scottish People, 1680-1830*, 1961; David Daiches, *The Paradox of Scottish Culture*, 1964; Douglas Young, *Edinburgh in the Age of Sir Walter Scott*, 1965.

   Qoutations from fiction are taken from the most common good edition, *The Ettrick Shepherd's Tales*, two vols., 1886, which follows the text of *Tales and Sketches, by the Ettrick Shepherd*, six vols., 1837, with the exceptions of *The Three Perils of Man*, where reference is to the edition of 1972; *The Three Perils of Women*, 1822 edition; *The Justified Sinner*, 1947 edition; and other short stories not collected in 1837, where reference is made to the originally published text in the appropriate periodical. Quotations from poetry are from *The Works of the Ettrick Shepherd*, two vols., ed. Thomson, 1865, vol. II.

   The dates of stories and poems will be found in the list of Hogg's works at the end.

2. Hogg thought he was born 25 January 1772—Burns's birthday, but the parish register gives 9 December 1770 for his baptism. See *Simpson*, n.p. 5.

3. James Hogg, *The Domestic Manners and Private Life of Sir Walter Scott*, 1834; this quotation (p. 53) and others from the 1909 edition.

4. G. H. Gerrould, *The Ballad of Tradition*, 1932, p. xi and p. 7.

5. *Tales*, vol. I, p. 207.

6. Throughout his *Scottish Literature; its Character and Influence*, 1919.

7. In a letter from Hogg's brother William to James Gray in 1813, quoted *Strout*, p. 8.

8. *Batho*, p. 35. She argues that Hogg's footnote "beautiful old rhyme," "The heron flew East," with its memory of Christ as a wounded knight, is in fact a "relic of the medieval allegory of the passion."

9. *Tales*, vol. II, p. 251.

10. In a letter to Scott of 1802 quoted in *Batho*, pp. 26-27.

11. Anne Grant, *Letters from the Mountains,* 1806. Dougal Graham, the "skellat bellman of Glasgow," and most popular of the eighteenth century makers of chapbook stories; *Collected Writings,* ed. G. McGregor, 1883. Robert Wodrow, *The Sufferings of the Church of Scotland,* 1721-2.
12. *Tales,* vol. I, p. 2.
13. *Tales,* vol. I, p. 39.
14. *Tales,* vol. I, p. 28.
15. *Domestic Manners,* p. 75 ff.
16. *Domestic Manners,* p. 70.
17. *Tales,* vol. I, p. 490.
18. *Tales,* vol. I, p. 99.
19. *Tales,* vol. II, p. 326.
20. *Tales,* vol. I, p. 314.
21. *The Justified Sinner,* p. 4.
22. The comment of his 1865 minister editor, J. Thomson, p. 128.
23. *Domestic Manners,* p. 91.
24. *Domestic Manners,* p. 63.
25. Margaret Oliphant, *Annals of a Publishing House; William Blackwood and his Sons,* 1898, vol. I, p. 324.
26. *Blackwood's Magazine,* March 1818, vol. II, p. 654.
27. Oliphant, vol. I, p. 329.
28. *Blackwood's Magazine,* August 1821, quoted in *Strout,* p. 223, William Chambers.
29. *Memoir of Robert Chambers,* 1872, pp. 247-254.

CHAPTER TWO

POETRY AND DRAMA:
Scottish Pastorals (1801) to
Dramatic Tales (1817)

"THOUGH HOGG'S POETRY brought him a considerable reputation, few of his poems claim the attention of the modern reader, and none compare with the best of his prose."[1] Thus Louis Simpson concluded his study of Hogg's poetry in 1962, after two excellent chapters analysing his poetic strengths and weaknesses. The only other significant modern commentator on Hogg's poetry has been Douglas Mack. After admitting the justice of re-establishing Hogg as novelist, he argues that "a re-examination of Hogg's achievement as a poet seems overdue." He concedes that Hogg "wrote far too much verse," drowning the best poems in his determination to follow literary fashions, and spoiling his undoubted Ballad gift by being diffuse, as in his 732-line "Mary Scott" of *The Queen's Wake,* founded on the 156-line "The Gay Goss-Hawk" of Scott's *Minstrelsy of the Scottish Border* (1802-3).

Conveniently enough for the overall argument of this study that Hogg is at his best a teller of prose tales, most of his more ambitious, "made" poems clearly fall into the period 1807-1814, with his *Dramatic Tales* appearing in 1817. Thus it can be seen that to a considerable extent Hogg developed *through* his poetry and drama into the novelist of *The Brownie of Bodsbeck* and that great period 1818-24 in which he wrote his major fiction. While I accept that Hogg's poetic creativity was far from exhausted by 1814, with his two volumes of *Jacobite Relics* to come, his *Songs* in 1831, and *A Queer Book* of longer poems in 1832, nevertheless Hogg himself argued that 1817 marked a turning-point for him:

> . . . since the poetical part of these dramas [*Dramatic Tales*] excited no interest in the public, I felt conscious that no poetry I should ever be able to write would do so. . . . So from that day to this, save now and then an idle song to beguile a leisure hour, I determined to write no more poetry.[2]

With the exception of his collections and his later finishing of *Queen Hynde*, begun earlier and put aside, Hogg stuck to this—if we allow that the "idle songs" were many and did not just beguile a leisure hour, but brought him in a steady income from magazines like *Blackwood's* and *Fraser's* till the end of his career. *Queen Hynde* apart, Hogg stopped having ambitions to write large, formal, discursive poems after the manner of Scott, Byron, Wordsworth and Wilson, and I believe that it was a logical step in his development as a writer that he should do so. The man reared on the concrete imagery, direct style, and storytelling form of the Ballads was bound to find himself out of tune with the poetic conventions of literary society. Where he succeeds, as Mack points out, is "when his object was to please himself rather than Edinburgh."[3] Hogg's poetry is good when he draws on his Ballad and story-telling background, telling rousing, fast-moving tales of "fierce loves and tender wars" on the Borders, or using his great love and knowledge of supernatural legends to create either racy, comic and earthy fantasies or haunting and occasionally lyrically beautiful descriptions of transitions from earth to heaven or fairyland. Out of these inspirations too come his best short verses and songs, whether they be dressed as Jacobite exhortations or simple, domestic, personal utterances.

The unusual exception to this pattern is the astonishing gift of poetic parody which produced the best imitations we have of Scott, Wordsworth, Southey and the like in his *Poetic Mirror*. The answer to the question as to where a self-taught shepherd acquired such ability must surely lie in the very fact that he had to "latch on" to different poetic styles, since as an uneducated peasant he was very unsure of his own creative identity. His own Ballad tradition he regarded too lightly, and this under-estimation creating a kind of stylistic vacuum which he needed to fill, Hogg tried out the available styles of the day.

In looking at Hogg's development as a writer it cannot be stressed enough that his imitative gift played a crucial part. Paradoxically, his swift and sometimes uncanny ability to "hear" the unique and characteristic phrases and images of other writers which made him one of, if not the finest parodist of romantic poets in English, was also a curse, in that whenever he felt creatively unsure of himself, due to adverse criticism of previous work, he instinctively reacted by using this talent to copy successful writers of the time. Thus in fiction he imitated aspects of Scott, Jane Austen, Susan Ferrier and Lockhart and the Gothic school, to his own aesthetic disadvantage, and it is in his main poetic period, up till *The Brownie of Bodsbeck* in 1818, that we see this habit most clearly.

His first tiny collection, *Scottish Pastorals, Poems, Songs &c.* of 1801 imitated Ramsay—poorly. His second collection, *The Mountain Bard* (1807) derived from Scott's *Minstrelsy of the Scottish Border* (1802-3), since Hogg felt that he too knew Border Ballads, and could indeed write his own. The ten ballad imitations of *The Mountain Bard* are nevertheless far better poetry than much of his later work, simply because he worked effortlessly here in a tradition to which he belonged. Artlessly he tells us that he based "Sir David Graeme" on "The Twa Corbies" in Scott's *Minstrelsy,* or "The Pedlar" on the account of the best informed old people around Ettrick. "Gilmanscleugh" comes from "an ancient family tradition," or "Mess John" from "a very popular story about Ettrick Forest." It is also highly significant that Hogg is drawn in most cases to give long, story-telling notes after these narrative poems. He quite obviously loves his material, and is genuinely and simply transmitting it to us without much garnishing or attempt to translate it into a modern manner. Obviously too the *story* is what holds him most deeply, as the notes develop narrative points.

These are straightforward tales, broadly of two classes. On one hand there are rousing, fast moving stories of "fierce wars and tender loves" of the old Border families after the manner of "Jamie Telfer" or "Kinmont Willie," and on the other there are Ballads of wraiths, simply telling of death of the real person elsewhere. The virtues of both are exactly those of the Ballads, although the reader will find an overall effect eventually of *pastiche.* For example, "Sir David Graeme" is a not unworthy rewriting of "The Twa Corbies," but it goes on far too long, and "stretches" the concise images and reflections of the original, as when the lady finds dead Sir David.

> There wasna sic een on the Border green
> As the piercing een o' Sir David Graeme;
> She glisked wi' her ee where those een should be
> But the raven had been there afore she came.[4]

Similarly close in spirit to its original "Wife of

Usher's Well," but somehow not quite compressing its vivid and eerie imagery enough is "The Wife of Crowle," where the mother sees her drowned boy.

> His form still grew, and the flame burnt blue
> I stretched out my arm to embrace;
> But he turned his dead eye, so hollow and dry
> And so wistfully gazed in my face. . . .[5]

There is of course an immediate loss of authority with the use of English, and even in this unpretentious set of Ballad-exercises one sees what is to be the main reason why Hogg could never really succeed as a poet, what Louis Simpson analysed accurately as "the uncertainty of Hogg's use of language."[6] Scott's English poems, albeit creating a fashion for Scottish scenes and characters, had "relegated the vernacular to second place and falsified those traditions which are embodied in the vernacular."[7] And unlike Fergusson and Burns, of whom David Daiches says that they "achieved success only when they repudiated the poetic tradition of the literati,"[8] Hogg never repudiated this tradition. Even when closest to his own, stronger tradition he too frequently and fatally allows the flavour of literary English to creep in.

> The sun had drunk frae Kielder fell
> His beverage o' the morning dew . . .[9]

or

> Amazement kythed in the shepherd's face,
> His mouth to open wide began . . .[10]

or

> Though the tender scion's woundit
> By a reptile's pois'nous twine,
> Must the noxious weeds around it
> In its ruin all combine?[11]

or

> Sternies blush, an' hide your faces!
> Veil thee, moon, in sable hue!
> Else thy locks, for human vices
> Soon will dreep wi' pity's dew.[12]

Admittedly these are glaring and unusual examples, but they are the extremes of a habit of using a layer of English phrases and words like "frenzied" and "hectic," "lubrick" or "voluptuary" which actually destroy the vigour and authenticity of the Scots. At its least destructive it merely causes the reader to make a slight reservation as he enjoys the rest, as in the eerie opening to "The Pedlar":

> 'Twas late, late, on a Saturday's night,
> The moon was set an' the wind was lown;
> The lazy mist crap down frae the height,
> An the dim blue lowe glimmered laigh on the down. . . .[13]

Hogg has decided here to moderate the strength of his Scots considerably in "night" and "height" and "downe," but the intrusive image/word is "lazy," which one feels is not used in any Scots sense or sound. But it almost works here, and with the much worse excesses of this kind to come, credit should be given to the poem for its more typical racy, vivid Scots, and the swift-moving story. The murdered pedlar is seen on this late night, "when the foxes did howl," with his green (and therefore ominous) pack on his back.

> "O where are ye gaun, ye beggarly loun?
> Ye's nouther get lodging nor sale frae me!"
> He turned him about, an' the blude it ran down,
> An his throat was a' hackered, an' ghastly was he.

36

Then staight wi' a sound he sank i' the ground,
An' a fire-flaught out o' the place did flee!
To try a bit prayer the laird clappet down,
As flat an' as feared as a body could be . . .[14]

"If a person could once succeed in the genuine ballad
style, his muse was adequate for any other," Hogg
thought.[15] He never did manage completely to recapture the spareness and economy of the original form,
but it is true that his best original poetry is in this
form, be it serious, as "The Pedlar," or more often
comic. The major development in Hogg's poetry seems
to me to be towards the achievement of a personal,
earthy and ironic tone which reconciles the reader
to the incredible events of poems like "The Witch of
Fife" or "May of the Moril Glen." The origins of
this—*pace* Simpson—can be seen in two poems of this
collection, "The Fray of Elibank" and "Willie Wilkin."
In the first there is the comic, reductive tone, and in
the second Hogg begins to explore that rich treasure-
house of Border legends of the "other landscape" which
produces his finest work. "The Fray of Elibank" is
hardly in "romantic manner," as Simpson argues, but
is a trial effort at the kind of material which *The Three
Perils of Man* brings to fruition. It is in fact an anti-
romantic poem, since its point is that when young
Scott of Harden is captured by old Juden Murray, his
father's reaction is hardly conventionally romantic:

Though Harden was grieved, he durst venture nae
   further
But left his poor son to submit to his fate.
"If I lose him," quo' he, "I may chance get another,
But never again wad get sic an estate."[16]

Similarly unromantic is Murray's ultimatum, to

young captive Will, all the more ironic for its "fatherly" conversational good-humour.

> "Now, Will, as ye're young, an' I hope ye may mend,
> On the following conditions I grant ye your life;—
> That ye be mair wary, an' auld Juden's friend,
> An' accept o' my daughter there Meg for your wife."[17]

Did Stevenson know this poem? Certainly Hogg's account of the hero's noble resolve to perish giving way in the sight of his imminent death compares favourably with "The Sire de Malatroit's Door," especially as Hogg's version doesn't allow the hero the "out" of a beautiful bride-to-be:

> Now Meg was but thin, an' her nose it was lang,
> An her mou' it was muckle as ane could weel be; . . .
> But Willie now fand he was fairly i' the wrang
> That marriage an' death were twa different things—
> "What matter," quo' he, "though her nose it be lang?
> For noses bring luck, an' it's welcome that brings."[18]

The parallel with *The Three Perils of Man* extends further than tone, for like that novel the poem is a sly "compliment" to Scott and his ancestors. Out of such unions and unromantic realism comes "mony a brave fellow"—including Scott. And Hogg's own ancestors are in the poem, as the fiercest allies of the Scotts against Juden, "the Wild Boar of Fauldshope" being Juden's greatest fear: "I like that cursed Hogg ill;/Nae devil in hell but I rather wad see," taking part in action described in deliberately deflating terms.

> Brave Robin o' Singlee was cloven through the brain,
> An' Kirkhope was woundit, an' young Baillylee.
> Wi' Juden, baith Gatehope an' Plora were slain,
> An' auld Ashiesteel gat a cut on the knee.[19]

This is hardly "exploits of legendary names, descriptions of stage scenery, and glorification of Scotland,"[20] and is deliberately *against* the ethos of *Marmion*. The point is important, because in this poem one sees the beginning of that collection of fine, rollicking, anti-romantic riots presided over by a Lord of Misrule. If one adds to this tone the subject matter of "Willie Wilkin," a tale of a famous Michael Scott-like warlock, with his "thirty coal black steeds" in "yon kirk-yard/where graves are green and low," steeds which turn out to be phantoms of smoke and "sulph'ry wind" (therefore hellish), with "brimstone air" with "thunders and fireflaughts" destroying the intruder, we are firmly in the country and the language of "The Witch of Fife," *The Hunt of Eildon,* and *The Three Perils of Man.*

But development of these important strands in his poetry had to wait for another six years. In between, Hogg came to Edinburgh, started *The Spy,* and brought out *The Forest Minstrel,* collecting his songs contributed for some years now to *The Scots Magazine.* There seems to me in these songs to be little development discernible here—or at any point in Hogg's career. The achievement of a good song seems so much a matter of chance, as Simpson says:

When form, language, and subject fused, as they did on rare occasions his poems seemed happy accidents, or, as he would say, the result of inspiration.[21]

Consideration of his songs can thus be left till after our survey of the poetry that *did* develop, for there are triumphant examples in *The Queen's Wake* of 1813 of Hogg's full discovery of two tones, dealing with different kinds of traditional supernatural.[22] On the evidence of "The Witch of Fife" and "Old David" alone, Hogg is entitled to call himself "King of the Mountain and Fairy School."

I do not think I can improve on the discussions of Mack and Simpson respectively on *The Queen's Wake*, and I refer the reader who wishes fuller analysis of the poem to them. I agree with Mack that the poem as a whole is a failure. It has a happy idea behind it, that of a festival poetry to celebrate Mary Queen of Scots' arrival in Scotland. The festival takes place over three days, being a competition of bards from all over Scotland. Each declaims his narrative poem, and the device enables Hogg to indulge in his love of different "hats" and styles while at the same time preserving a kind of unity for the whole—always a difficult problem for him.

Many of the poems can be dismissed as Gothic, melodramatic and affected in language. Rizzio's song, "Malcolm of Lorn," is packed with trite sentiments like, "But never can a mother's love/From her own offspring part," (which, on the evidence of *The Justified Sinner* and many other Hogg stories is demonstrably untrue!) and "Break not her fond heart, gentle Malcolm, O stay!" It descends into bathos, through carelessness ("Or pleasures and virtues alternately borrow/As Malcolm of Lorn and fair Ann of Glen-ora"!) or over-reaching ("the curlew conned her wild bravura"). The comment on it in the intervening, linking commentary between poems, a device like that of the Host's comments in *The Canterbury Tales,* is interesting in that it illustrates perfectly what Hogg does at several points throughout. He betrays his own lack of confidence in the very poems he has himself written. He "covers" for many of the poems by suggesting afterwards as with "The Witch of Fife," that the bard is "crazy" and that "his song he holds

at nought/"an idle strain! a passing thought." This
is a very human symptom of unsureness, to disguise
how much one feels for one's efforts by diminishing
them in public—but Hogg was to show the symptoms
and betray the offspring (as with his savaging of *The
Three Perils of Man*) till he died. Now, after the first
song, Hogg describes how "that affected gaudy rhyme/
the querulous keys and changing chime,/. . . That song
so vapid, artful, terse [*sic*]/Should ere compete with
Scottish verse." We can be sure that Hogg did not
deliberately start with a bad poem, but this is his "out."
Worse is "Young Kennedy," with its Gothic melo-
drama, with Matilda who indulges in "painful delect-
able dreams" and its demonic destroyer Kennedy, the
"nursling of misery," who suffers a fate comparable to
"The Fate of McGregor," another betrayer of innocent
womanhood, or "Abbot McKinnon," whose taking up
with ladies is his undoing. This last shows Hogg closest
to that habit that Daiches rightly disliked in Ramsay,
that "schoolboy snigger."[23] Hogg *is* sometimes guilty
of bad taste but not in his frank, honest way the
literati disliked in his earthy stories of peasant life.
Sometimes though, as here and in stories like the third
of *The Perils of Women* he is not frank, and furtively
hints at his meaning, like the Ramsay of the additional
stanzas to *Christis Kirk on the Green*. What he is
saying is that "when the Abbot's away, the monks will
play"; but instead of being direct, Hogg insinuates:

> Then they turned their eyes to the female dome
> And thought of the nuns till the abbot came home . . .
> And the laugh rings through the sacred dome,
> For still the abbot is not come home. . . .[24]

The entire poem is an extended implication that the
"stranger youth" who "lodged with the Abbot by

day and by night" is his mistress, and the occasional vivid glimpses of Fingal's cave do not blow away the cloying atmosphere.

Imitating a healthier vein in Ramsay, that of his "Vision," is "King Edward's Dream," with Edward seeing Wallace as Guardian of Scotland. There is a certain power of poetic peroration about this, and it is Hogg's best extended and formal nationalist poem, besides which his later "Wallace" is empty noise. There are a number of respectable poems in *The Queen's Wake,* but usually they are in the Ballad form, like "Glen Avin," "Earl Walter" and "Mary Scott," which do not have the vitality of Scots within them, but tell workmanlike stories of *The Mountain Bard* kind in standard English. One of the main reasons for the overall failure of *The Queen's Wake* must surely be that only one of the twelve poetic tales is told in Scots, which is surprising, since Hogg had ostensibly created the Wake as a *national* celebration.

It is the tale in Scots that is the only completed unified masterpiece. All recent critics agree that "The Witch of Fife" is one of Hogg's finest poems. It fully develops the vein begun in "The Fray of Elibank," extending it into the wilder regions of faery. Both Simpson and Mack give the poem excellent and extensive review, and I echo Mack's verdict:

The "Witch of Fife" is rooted in the distinctive feeling of the old Scottish peasantry for the supernatural, a feeling which Lord David Cecil had described as being "at once homely and Gothic, earthy and fantastic, at times grotesquely comic, but shot through with an authentic thrill of supernatural terror.[25]

The tale of the old witch whose husband follows her

to the Bishop of Carlisle's wine cellar has all the archetypal simplicity of plot that is the essence of the great folk-tale. It is in the tradition of Dunbar's "Dance of the Seven Deadly Sins" in its comic pace, and Burns's "Tam o' Shanter" in its colour and humour, and thus in the mainstream of the tradition of great Scottish poetry. But it also has its own unique attitude. There is a Ballad toughness of tone, which was intended by Hogg to reach a climax in the death of the old man at the stake—till Walter Scott sent his wife to rescue him! [26] There is a feeling for environment, with landscape taking part in the reign of misrule, that conveys a cosmic sense of a topsy-turvy dance of nature, together with a *sweep* of imagination that makes Hogg supreme when it comes to his frequent descriptions of wild, supernatural sky-rides. These can cross Scotland in an instant, as in *The Three Perils of Man*, the universe in slightly longer time, as in *The Pilgrims of the Sun*, or carry a balloon to the moon with its drunk shepherd declaiming deliriously on his Glenlivet and the moon's beauty. Hogg also has a talent undeveloped in Burns for subjugating the topography of Scotland to his comic vision, as with the picture of the witch drinking "fra the horns that never grew" on the Lomond hills. It is this familiar landscape that dances with superb fun and gusto to the wee, wee man's flute:

> It rang se sweit through the green Lommond
> That the nycht-winde lowner blew;
> And it soupit alang the Loch Leven
> And wakinit the white sea-mew.
>
> It rang se sweit through the green Lommond
> Se sweetly but se shill

That the wezilis laup out of their mouldy holis
And dancit on the mydnycht hill.

The corby craw cam gledgin near,
The ern gede veeryng bye;
And the troutis laup out of the Leven Loch
Charmit with the melody.[27]

And in a comic sense Hogg fulfils McDiarmid's
requirement in *The Drunk Man Looks at the Thistle*
that Scotland should be part of a larger world and
destiny, as he expands his canvas to take in, effortlessly,
the Norroway Sea, Lapland, and the international
festival of witches and warlocks. He fully sustains that
beauty of imagery, that peculiar fusion of the grotesque
and the tender, the descriptive and the narrative,
throughout. For once, and in his poetry, once only,
Hogg does not put a foot wrong, and the dance is
sustained to the magnificent end.

There is one final serious point of issue about this
poem that I must take up with Simpson. He argues
that "the Witch of Fife is not typical of Hogg's
writings of the supernatural . . . his usual practice is
quite different; it is to relate 'uncanny' occurrences
in the course of a realistic tale."[28] This is demonstrably
not true, as a reading of "Old David" in the *Wake*
will show, or more significantly, a reading of "May
of the Moril Glen," "The Guid Grey Katte," "The
Good Man of Alloa" and "Lytill Pynkie" will establish.
Indeed, Simpson's comment ignores the fact that in
all these Hogg deliberately followed the precedent of
"The Witch of Fife," trying with varying success to
recapture its magic. Since they are all derivative from
it, we should here consider this "school of the Witch
of Fife" although they are later poems. The finest of
them, as Alexander Scott has pointed out,[29] is "May of

the Moril Glen" (1827). With complete control of comic tone Hogg tells of this mysterious, beautiful maid who causes all men who see her to fall hopelessly in love. Like "The Fray of Elibank," its irony is not blatantly obvious, and the "skimmer" of Hogg's poetry could miss the superb fun of this and the similar poems by failing to catch the tone, which intends the reader to "reverse" his usual response. The real achievement is in the delicate balance of Hogg's rollicking ironic humour with hauntingly beautiful supernatural background. It is amazing how he can juxtapose beautiful descriptions of May and her palfrey of snowy hue, her rainbow mantle, her eyes—"The lightning that shot from her eyne,/flickered like elfin brand"—her cloud of amber brown hair, and her hawk, all presented with crystal clarity and an obvious love of the straightforward beauty of the subject, with the farce of the comic wooers. She may be limpidly described as "the fairest flower of mortal men," but, unwittingly, she is "a devil among the men" (and Hogg, as in *The Justified Sinner* and all his supernatural tales, means that "devil" to carry implications).

> For nine of them sticket themselves for love
> And ten louped in the main,
> And seven-and-thirty brake their hearts
> And never loved women again.[30]

This is Hogg on his surest ground, that of *The Three Perils of Man,* using the anti-romantic tone he loves with restraint, enriched with the variety and wonder of his folk-lore. Again, the natural world plays its part, as we are introduced to May's ewes, "stotts, and sturdy steers/and blithesome kids enew," her snow-white bull, her geese and ganders, her peacocks, and, delightfully, her chickens:

> And she had cocks with curled kaims
> And hens, full crouse and glad,
> That chanted in her own stack-yard,
> and cackillit and laid like mad.[31]

O happy hens, to belong to such an enchantress! For "where her minnie gat all that gear . . . The Lord in heaven he knew full well/But nobody knew but him." She may not be devil, but she is unearthly, if pure. Hogg never descends to a bald statement, but, in a way that no other Scottish writer can, leaves his May an enigma to the last, as maybe "found in a fairy ring," maybe born of the fairy queen, or even a witch. . . .

Meanwhile, the gasping for breath and the rivers of tears of the love-lorn continue unabated, till, the King himself hearing of it, he determines that he will find out whether she be witch or no, and if she is, to burn her. But he is no more proof than his sixteen knights who "lay gasping on the plain." And in the picture of the King reduced to tantrums, lying on the grass, drumming his feet and pulling up clods:

> "What ails, what ails my royal liege?
> Such grief I do deplore"[32]

—there is real reductive humour, a valid puncturing of pomposity, which so often runs to seed in the uncontrolled clowning of some of his tales. A real friendship of letters in Edinburgh could have based sound advice to Hogg on this, pointing out how the *tone* of this poem unifies the two aspects in contrast with the incongruous and uncontrolled serious and comic aspects of *The Bridal of Polmood*.

With the King of Scotland crazed in love the poem reaches its climax, as May promises to wed the first widower amongst her followers. The race is on:

And seventy-seven wedded dames,
As fair as e'er were born
The very pride of all the land
Were dead before the morn . . .
While burial met with burial still,
And jostled by the way.[33]

There is an echo of "The Daemon Lover" in the end, as May, forced to abandon Scotland, vanishes in a splendid, haunting scene, where seven golden chariots take her to a ship in the Firth of Forth. Its masts are of beaten gold, its sails of silk, and rainbows surround it. The very dolphins flee before it, and "the black-guard seals they yowlit for dread" as the uncanny ship seems to float on the air rather than the sea:

And away, and away went the bonny ship,
Which man did never more see;
But whether she went to heaven or hell,
Was ne'er made known to me . . .[34]

Identical in tone to these is "The Gude Greye Katt," Hogg's parody of himself in his *Poetic Mirror.* He uses his irritating pseudo-antique Scots for most of these poems, an imitation of the middle Scots of the Old Makars, which boils down to using *quh* for *wh, -it* for *-ed,* and the like. It is of course not real Middle Scots, but the reader quickly learns how to strip the veneer from the poem as he reads. "The Gude Greye Katt," really the Queen of Fairies, takes an unwilling, lustful bishop on a punitive jaunt through the milky way, and there is the same grotesque humour in the picture of his aerial antics, as he roars and prays his way above Dollar Law, with the oddly sinister accompaniment of the cat's purr, "like katt that hethe ane jollye mouse/Gaun murrying throu the hall." Like the wee, wee man's flute-playing, her song is so sweet that muircocks dance a ring of seven round the heather bell, foumarts jig, otters dance minuets, and the tup-hog waltzes with the ewe. The poem even has an additional level to "The Witch of Fife" or "May of the Moril Glen," in that irony which anticipates *The Justified Sinner* lies behind the cat's reply to the bishop's plea not to drop him in the crater of Mount Etna. Like Gilmartin persuading Wringhim to kill Blanchard by pointing out that if he is good he will immediately exchange his place for a better, the cat says "with lychtsum air"

> You kno hevin is ane blissit place
> And all the prestis gang there . . .[35]

And his end is one of the most vivid of Hogg's comic nightmares.

> Doune went the Byschope, doune lyke leide,
> Into the hollowe nychte;
> His goune was flapping in the aire,
> Qhan he was out of sychte.
>
> They hearit him honyng doune the deep,
> Till the croone it dyed awaye;
> It wase lyke the stoune of ane great bom-be
> Gaun soundyng throu the day.[36]

No one but Hogg could have chosen "honyng" for the sound of the far-falling bishop, or used "croon," with all its mellifluous associations, for such a grotesque death-cry. The metaphor of the sound of the bumble-bee, usually reserved for the evocation of a sleepy summer's day, is brilliantly and originally used to complete the effect of the two earlier terms. It is a pity that Hogg partly spoiled the superb climax by having the cat explicitly reveal that she is the Queen of the

48

Fairies come to protect the seven daughters of the Laird of Blain from worldly danger by spiriting them off for the "Tam Lin" period of seven years. The passage of this time and the joy of the father's meeting with his daughters is inappropriate to the spirit of comic extravaganza which has dominated hitherto.

Similar extravaganza and riot dominates "Lyttil Pynkie." Pinkie is, like the cat, an unearthly guardian, who leads wicked baron, chaplain and finally even minister Mess John a dance, literally. Like the topsy-turvy caused by May and the riot of the other poems of the group is the unstoppable, enchanted dance that her sweet song begins, and there is the same breathless and vivid humour present in the antics. Not as good, but still a vital member of the group is "the Gude man of Alloa," with a miser being taken on a weird flight over the oceans by a bonnie maid on a gray palfrey, yet another variant of the enchantress from the "other world," with what the reader will recognise by now as Hogg's hallmarks in the antics and reversals of animals and nature.[37]

The truth is that Hogg created many poems *and* novels and short stories from this rich area of diablerie and fantasy. *The Hunt of Eildon, The Three Perils of Man,* "The Witches of Traquair," "Dr. David Dale's Account of a Grand Aeriel Voyage," "A Story of the Black Arts," and many other stories continue in prose what Hogg began in "The Witch of Fife." I would suggest that far from not being typical of Hogg's writings of the supernatural, that the poem first high-lights what is to become the richest vein of all in Hogg's work.

Impressive in its echoes of *Sir Orfeo,* with passages of lovely and haunting description of a white-and-green-clad fairy band, is "Old David." It is different from "The Witch of Fife" in mood, and moves closer still to *The Three Perils of Man* in that it blends "The Fray of Elibank" element of folk history of great Border families with the fairyland material, linking for the first time "fierce wars and tender loves" with the supernatural spectrum of bizarre creatures. Old David, fierce and grim Border warrior, is precursor of Sir Ringan Redhough, and like Ringan is unhappily involved with enchantment, as he hears the windblown tinkle of the silver bells of the lovely fairy band. Hogg manages marvellously to convey the paradoxically chilling effect on David of the bell:

> But as the tinkling sound came nigh,
> Old David's heart beat wondrous high.
> He thought of riding on the wind;
> Of leaving hawk and hern behind;
> Of sailing lightly o'er the sea,
> In mussel-shell to Germany;
> Of revel raids by dale and down;
> Of lighting torches at the moon;
> Or through the sounding spheres to sing,
> Borne on the fiery meteor's wing;
> ... And then he thought—O! dread to tell! —
> Of tithes the fairies pay to hell! [38]

David sees that they have a captive maiden of earth, and with his seven sons, determines to try Rippon steel against her captors. Hogg has no rivals in describing adventures like these, as long as he follows tradition and presents his material directly and simply. Oddly, the reader is saddened by David's easy victory against the fairies, and at the carnage that ensues. Here Hogg states a theme which almost takes on the stature of myth, here and in later poems like "Superstition" (1814) and the beautiful "Verses Addressed to

. . . Lady Anne Scott of Buccleuch" (1818). He notes in *The Queen's Wake* that "the fairies have now totally disappeared; and it is a pity they should, for they seem to have been the most delightful little spirits that ever haunted the Scottish dells."[39] With Hogg's other statements on the subject, like his account of how his grandfather was the last man to see them in the region, we realise that Hogg is being serious, and specific. He means *fairies,* not witches, or the devil, or the supernatural generally. Indeed, his note goes on to say that in the present day witches are even more believed in than ever before. And in his lament for the passing of the fairies one is tempted to see him coming as near as he ever does to a kind of symbolism for older Scotland. There is certainly the quality of profound and sorrowful elegy that haunts the pages of *The Three Perils of Man* as it describes the passing of the last really great wizard of Scotland, Sir Michael Scott.

> E'er since, in Ettrick's glens so green
> Spirits, though there, are seldom seen;
> And fears of elf, and fairy raid,
> Have like a morning dream decayed. . . .
> True, some weak shepherds, gone astray,
> As fell the dusk of Hallow-day,
> Have heard the tinkling sound aloof,
> And gentle tread of horses' hoof. . . .[40]

Hogg, "banished" from Ettrick to Edinburgh at this time, finished this fine poem with a lovely invocation of Ettrick, filled with longing and a recognition that it is woven into his deepest being. The intermingling of the lament for the fairies and for Ettrick strikes a chord of rare beauty in Hogg's longer poems, found in only two other poems. In "Superstition," he pays moving tribute to his mother's gift of vision and legend to him. Here in poetry is the reckoning of the endless debt for fairies, spirits and seers that her tales and Ballads gave Hogg, even down to the "grave of suicide, upon the brow of the bleak mountain, withered all and gray. . . ." We have reason to be grateful to that amazing woman for so much, including, it seems, the basic idea of *The Justified Sinner*. Again Hogg ties in the personal loss with the fairies, almost as though they represent the spirit of yesteryear:

> —Woe is me!
> That thou and all thy spectres are outworn,
> For true devotion wanes away with thee;
> All thy delirious dreams are laughed to scorn,
> While o'er our hills has dawned a cold saturnine morn . . .
> All these are gone—the days of vision o'er;
> The bard of fancy strikes a tuneless string . . .[41]

The finest expression of this blend of personal loss of country innocence is without doubt the "Verses . . . to . . . Anne Scott of Buccleuch," daughter of the late Duchess of Buccleuch, beloved in Hogg's memory both for her goodness generally and the fact that it was her dying wish that ensured Hogg his return to Ettrick in 1815 by placing him rent-free for life in Altrive Lake Farm. The poem, too complete to spoil by excerpt, is filled with a sincerity motivated by the memory of "steps where once an angel trod" in which Lady Anne now follows. It is an *apologia* for his love of mystic lore, covenanting traditions (for the Buccleughs were Episcopalian), and an evocation of ancient, spirit-filled Ettrick:

> . . . note the stars rise one by one;—
> Just then, the moon and day-light blending,

52

> To see the fairy bands descending,
> Wheeling and shivering as they came,
> Like glimmering shreds of human frame . . .
> Such scenes, dear Lady, now no more. . . .[42]

"Old David" was the first of these uncanny evocations of the vanishing world of fairyland. After the disappointment at the lack of success of his novels, Hogg was to write less and less frequently with this real sensitivity—unique, I believe, in Scottish poetry—on these topics. It is significant that a poem of 1830, "The Origin of the Fairies," while still possessing the power to re-create that atmosphere that Keats caught in "La Belle Dame sans Merci," merges this atmosphere with a "May of the Moril Glen" comic resolution. Here the knight who has fallen for the fairy maiden and, like Tam Lin or Thomas lived with the fairies, is confronted when back in the real world with not just one maiden and child, but, beautiful in gold and green,

> Seven dames all lovely as morns of May
> With fourteen babies in a ring . . .[43]

There is an echo of the earlier lament for the passing of the fairies in the Seven Weird Sisters prophecy/command that their fairy children should abandon fair Scotland when "psalms and prayers are nightly heard," and when the landscape grows too busy and worldly for them. But the fineness of mood has gone, with the mixing of the farcical and the faery. To this extent the poem illustrates perfectly that in poetry at least Hogg's "development" involved an unfortunate move away from his sources of true inspiration.

Douglas Mack has argued that critics have not

appreciated the true achievement and meaning of "Kilmeny," one of the finest of the poems in "The Queen's Wake." It is *not,* he claims, a poem about fairies, since Kilmeny is taken not to fairyland but to heaven, and "the land of spirits is never called fairyland in the poem, nor are its inhabitants ever called fairies . . . they are very different beings from the fairies of . . . 'Old David'."[44] Although, as so often in all Hogg's poetry and fiction, the crucial Ballads of "Tam Lin" and "Thomas the Rhymer" are a base for the poem, they are merely a starting point, and Mack believes that Hogg created a myth entirely different in its significance, being an intensely Christian poem which echoes Isaiah's vision of the New Jerusalem. The only weakness of a poem otherwise comparable to the great medieval English poem "Pearl," and "the most important religious poem to have been produced in Scotland since the Midde Ages," is that part set in heaven, due firstly to the impossibility of a human mind conceiving heaven, and secondly to the "chauvinistic account of the terrors of the French revolution and a pageant of the life of Mary Queen of Scots." (These last two episodes form the vision of the lion and the eagle.)

John Mair goes further. He sees criticism as too obsessed with the vision, which he interprets as the representation of the reign of Queen Mary, followed by a description of Scotland's seventeenth-century troubles, and argues that more important is analysis of the opening and closing sections, which should stress Kilmeny's affinity with Nature and her uniqueness. "She is eternal. She is the truth." Linking her as a symbolic figure with the "nationalistic enthusiasm" which "pervades the description of Scotland" in the central sections, Mair sees Kilmeny as "Nature, having become truth and infinity, having been shown to be Scottish, and finally being seen in Scotland instilling peace and harmony into the predatory world of wild creatures . . . the true spirit of Scotland."[45]

While agreeing that "Kilmeny" is a poem with more than usual Christian atmosphere and less than usual pagan or fairy references, I am sceptical of separating it so completely in terms of achievement and theme from the body of his poetry. It is the finest of a number of poems which are "purer" in their religious themes and christianity than Hogg's usual mingling of the Christian and pagan. Hogg in the later "Pilgrims of the Sun" tries to blow up the "Kilmeny" situation into a long poem, and much later in "Elen of Reigh" (1829) and "A Greek Pastoral" (1830) he was to return to the themes of a pure maiden too good for this world and transportation through the agency of heavenly creatures. But if one looks closely at these one finds that the degree of Christian reference varies slightly but significantly. "Elen of Reigh" is indeed the purest Christian of them all, and there is no trace of fairyland in that poem. Kilmeny is like her, but comes back from wherever she has been with that "bonny snood of the birk sae green" taken from the same place as the hats of the birk of the three sons of "The Wife of Usher's Well." Kilmeny has been "where the cock never crew." The poem thus moves its terms of reference slightly away from the totally Christian framework towards the Ballad world which allows Christian and pagan imagery and meaning to mingle, as in the tale *The Hunt of Eildon,* where two maidens of "Kilmeny" purity and Christian piety are nevertheless permitted powers of enchantment of fellow-humans, turning them into animals or birds, and can themselves

55

turn into white hounds at will. Christianity and fairy-land merge easily together. But in "A Greek Pastoral" Hogg takes the "Kilmeny" situation in a different direction still. He has the maiden "teleported" again, but this time merely from "a distant eastern clime" to "proud Olympus," to meet a Scottish Soldier who in turn has been transported by "an old grey man." There are many echoes of "Kilmeny." The girl is a "virgin of peerless fame," trusts in her God (Christian? Her dead father's spirit lies at "his saviour's feet"); is at one with "woodland wild" and nature, and falls into a deep sleep before her journey. But this time Elves conduct her journey, although oddly they seem to be working for God and heaven, and odder still, with the end of making her Queen of Thessaly and finding her a Scottish mate!

The truth is that the theme of the virtuous maiden adopted and protected by heavenly spirits who may or may not employ fairy/elvish/supernatural agents to assist them is one of Hogg's most recurrent themes in poetry, fiction and even in drama. In fiction he deals with it in *The Hunt of Eildon,* "Mary Burnet" (the beauty of which story depends, in total contrast to "Kilmeny" on the magnificent use of fairy imagery), and in Cherry's dream in *The Three Perils of Women,* to name but a few, and in drama, the unsuccessful but sometimes beautiful *The Haunted Glen.* I am thus reluctant to set "Kilmeny" apart *in kind* from these other works, although I grant it is superior in quality. Hogg himself thought "Elen of Reigh" "my master-piece, 'Kilmeny' not excepted," "*best I ever wrote*";[46] which argues that, although he realised that there was a Kilmeny theme, he was *not* in "Kilmeny" itself setting out to create a poem with a symbolism and level of interpretation different from the others. Hogg was *not* a symbolist like Scott or Stevenson or in any modern sense. Scott does use Jeannie Deans, the heart of real compassion and feeling in Midlothian and Scotland, as a symbol of moral truth and spiritual regeneration, and Stevenson does use Henry and James Ballantrae to represent the mutually destructive qualities present within the Scottish soul, but Hogg, belonging to a much older tradition, uses no such deliberate play on levels of meaning. True, one can argue that there are glimmerings of further meaning in his lament for the lost fairies of Scotland, or that Wat of Chapelhope in *The Brownie of Bodsbeck* stands for non-denominational, intuitive christian charity against Covenanting or Episcopalian bigotry, or that the conflict between Michael Scott the Wizard and the Friar in *The Three Perils of Man* represents Evil against Good, but these are arrangements of meaning which would emerge spontaneously from Hogg's very nature. Hogg is no thinker, in formal or aesthetic terms, but a writer of vivid imagination, who conceives dramatic scenes with concrete clarity, who has sufficient range of ideas and expression to sustain his visions at an immediate level, and a dry, ironic, practical and reductive humour or a certain tenderness to further clothe them. I agree with Douglas Mack's view that the visions of "Kilmeny" are the weakest aspects, and they are the very parts of the poem where Hogg starts to "think," or to reveal his profound weaknesses as a political, moral commentator. His politics are naive, ranging from sentimental Jacobitism to unquestioning devotion to George IV and doctrinaire antagonism to Whigs and radicals, and his morality, though instinctively good-natured and compassionate, hardly, for all the conventional good sense of his *Lay Morals,* formalised in a way that would suggest an integrated view which could use Kilmeny as an embodiment of what he felt was departing from Scotland. The success of "Kilmeny" is, I believe, partly a happy accident; accident, in the sense that, apart from the naive choice of historical examples of human wickedness, Hogg introduced fewer of his usual conventional reflections in poems of this kind which celebrate maidenly virtue.

Nevertheless, if Kilmeny is not to be taken as a Jeannie Deans, or a "Chris Caledonia" (Chris Guthrie of *A Scots Quair* (1932-34)), John Mair is surely right to draw our attention to her harmonising influence, which is in complete contrast to the effect of the protagonists in the comic poems like "The Witch of Fife." Where these poems create topsy-turvy confusion in nature, with their Witches as Ladies of Misrule, Kilmeny a unifying presence, and with her birch-snood, has come, like the sons of the wife of Usher's Well, from the gates of paradise. The poem may be neither completely Christian vision or symbolic statement of Scotland's spiritual degeneration, but it has its own magnificent achievement in its beautiful realisation of an archetypal and ancient vision of transcendental spirit and beauty triumphing over place and time. It is universal and local simultaneously.

The Queen's Wake cannot be regarded as a success now. Based as it was on a falsification of the evidence of Mary Queen of Scots' *real* reaction to Scotland when she came,[47] it seems thereafter to "float" in a limbo-Scotland of Hogg's imagination, and there can be no possibility of our elevating Mary to the level of symbol, whereby she stands for an older, freer Scotland about to enter its tragic Reformation, even although the occasional references to the need for secret Catholic rites "close from the zealot's searching eyes" might suggest so. Hogg is merely making a local point about Mary. Louis Simpson speculated that in the awarding of the prizes Hogg was expressing something deeper, since the rejection of Rizzio's claim can be taken as representing the rejection of the presumptions of authority. "Is Hogg thereby revealing his own resentment of the authority of Tory Edinburgh? When he awards the prize to the Highland bard, and a consolatory prize to the shepherd, is he protesting on behalf of popular Scottish poetry?"[48] We can only speculate here, although I feel that increasingly Hogg was to embody his own feeling of being surrounded by a conspiracy of polite authority to cut off his every advance, and I will argue that Hogg's sense of an almost devilish plot through which he, as innocent victim, could not see, contributes real power to his *The Justified Sinner* and later stories.

The two best songs of *The Queen's Wake* are written in a mixture of Scots and English, but Hogg made the prize go to the "Young Kennedy," the Gothic horror story. Hogg's strength lay in writing about folk traditions, but it was to become increasingly obvious that he himself was not aware of this. In the next year, elated with the popular success of *The Queen's Wake,* he was to write two more long poems, *Mador of the Moor* and *The Pilgrims of the Sun.* He thought that *Mador* contained "my highest and most fortunate efforts in rhyme . . . in some of the descriptions of nature."[49] It is an unhappy re-telling of the legend of the "Gaberlunzie Man," the king who sometimes goes about as gypsy, but without the vitality and Scots of the original version. The poem was written at his hostess's request when he stayed in Athol, and Hogg may be right when he says in his introduction to the poem:

But aye when from the echoing hills I run,
My froward harp refuses to comply;
The nursling of the wild, The Mountain Bard am I.[50]

There is a half-truth here, that Hogg's background has a vital connection with his work; but that half-truth is simultaneously repudiated by the language Hogg uses to express it, since it is the language of the very tradition he rejected in Rizzio's "affected gaudy rhyme." Hogg never expresed clearly any dissatisfaction he may have felt with his models of Scott and Wilson.

The poem is in the worst Hogg vein, that in which he repeats the snigger of Ramsay, and fails to see the incongruity between language and action. The crude antics of the unheroic gypsy-king—

But he was out, and in-above-beneath,
Unhinging doors, and groping in the dark;
The hamlet matrons dread unearthly scathe
The matrons hide their heads, the watch-dogs bark
And all was noise and fright till matin . . .[51]

—stops us from feeling any involvement in the central love affair, and the sequel, the unmarried mother's ruin and wonderful redemption, takes the action into the kailyard world of Galt's *Sir Andrew Wylie* (1822), where any genuine genuine feeling for the peculiarly Scottish nature of the theme is falsified. To compare the treatment of unmarried motherhood in peasant surroundings—the reality of which Hogg must, as a shepherd, have been fully aware,—with William Alexander's description of the subject in "Baubie Hughie's Bastard Geet,"[52] from his *Life Among My Ain Folk* (1875), with all its harsh, but somehow compassionate realism, is to see how far Hogg has allowed his peasant realism and sense to desert him for phony models. It is immediately striking to see how the quality rises when he brings in the genuine traditions of the Borders, as when the mother, rejected and journeying with her babe at night, sees how

> From every crevice of the walls there looked
> Small elvish faces of malignity;
> And, oh, their gleaming eyes could ill be
> brooked . . . .[53]

—and doubly sad to see Hogg still in touch with his Ballad roots, but now abusing them. Hogg has a Palmer tell the mother his tale ("Oh, be his tale a warning youthful vice to shun") and shamelessly abuses the situation and words of the fine Ballad "The Cruel Mother" in it. The Ballad tells of the murdered, unearthly child who returns to accuse the mother as she comes out of the kirk. She at first does not realise its identity—

> O sweet babes, gin ye were mine
> Hey the rose and the linsie, O
> I'd clothe ye up in silk so fine
> Awa' by the green wood sidie, O.
>
> O Cruel mother, when we were thine
> Hey the rose and the linsie, O
> Ye didna prove tae us so kind
> Awa' by the green wood sidie, O.

Hogg has

> "Sweet babe," she simpered, with affected mien
> "Thou are a lovely boy; if thou wert mine
> I'd deck thee in the gold and diamond sheen,
> And daily bathe thee in the rosy wine . . .

"O lady of the proud unfeeling soul,
'Tis not three little months since I was thine;
And thou did'st deck me in the grave-cloth foul,
And bathe me in the blood—that blood was mine! "[55]

Analysis of the difference shows exactly how Hogg has strayed from home ground to alien. In the same year he strayed even further, with *The Pilgrims of the Sun,* which is interesting only in that it shows that success in a poem or song or parody for Hogg meant that he would ever after repeat the style and content in the vain hope of recapturing the glory of the original. "Kilmeny" is his precedent here. He extends her trip to take in the universe. I cannot improve on Simpson:

> . . . he transports the spirit of a mildly agnostic young lady into space, instructs her in theology, history and philosophy, and guides her on a tour of the planets.[56]

The theology is interesting only in that it reveals Hogg's religious tolerance and (very shallow and mild) tendency to free-thinking, while the rest of the intellectual effort that is expended in this, his most deliberately thoughtful poem, shows once and for all that Hogg is no thinker. It also shows him, right in the middle of his poetic career, still playing about in other poets' styles, using in turn the manner of Scott, Pope and Milton. The Milton imitation is clever, but the fact that Hogg used these styles for a major undertaking yields much more information about his basic insecurity of creative purpose than it does real poetry. It is not surprising that the following year saw the parodies of his poetic contemporaries in *The Poetic Mirror.* Hogg had the idea that a volume could be made up for his benefit by getting contributions from his contemporaries. Some agreed, but the scheme fell apart when Scott, to Hogg's great annoyance, refused. With the sense of fun that shortly produced "The Chaldee Manuscript," the letter in *Blackwood's* which would be put to good use in *The Justified Sinner,* Hogg wrote Scott's contribution for him—and Byron's, and Wordsworth's, Coleridge's, Southey's, and Wilson's. He even wrote a parody of himself. They are brilliant, and superb fun to read, especially the Wordsworth parodies in "The Stranger," "The Flying Tailor" and "James Rigg."

> A boy came from the mountains, tripping light
> With basket on his arm—and it appeared
> That there was butter there, for the white cloth,
> That over it was spread, not unobserved,
> In tiny ridges gently rose and fell,
> Like graves of children covered o'er with snow. . . .[57]

Hogg, before ever meeting Wordsworth and being insulted by him, has his revenge for all time in these wicked reductions. All Wordsworth's sonorous, prosy, almost bathetic moralising is made to crumble in Hogg's hands, all the more effectively because Hogg does not forget to put in poetry of which Wordsworth would not be ashamed. It is summed up in the end of "The Stranger," when, after the stranger's body has been discovered and given rise to long musing on principles of truth on the part of the poet, a chilling messenger halts his impressive discourse; the very birds are hushed, as the black shape journeys through the bowels of the deep.

> It was a tadpole—somewhere by itself
> The creature had been left, and there had come

Most timeously, by Providence sent forth,
To close this solemn and momentous tale.[58]

But, apart from "The Gude Greye Katt," these poems
are isolated, if very real achievements in Hogg's
development, concerning which all that they reveal
is how deeply he must have felt the need to learn what
constituted proper and socially acceptable poetic style.

Hogg's next considerable publication was his
Dramatic Tales of 1817. He seems to have started
trying his hand at drama about the time of *The Poetic
Mirror*. His confidence in his poetic abilities was
shaken, and, with the experience gathered from three
successful years (1811-1814) as secretary of the
Forum debating society, where he spoke weekly, his
thoughts turned naturally enough to a more public
form of literature. He had come off "with flying
colours" as speaker, and obviously believed that he
knew how to handle an audience.

> Private societies signify nothing; but a discerning
> public is a severe test, especially in a multitude,
> where the smallest departure from good taste . . .
> was sure to draw down disapproval, and where no
> good saying ever missed approbation and applause.[59]

The musical farce called *The Forum, a Tragedy for
Cold Weather* we have lost, but in 1817 Hogg collected
his other dramas into *Dramatic Tales*. The older
Hunting of Badlewe was modified to *The Profligate
Princes,* which is imitation Shakespeare, purporting to
be set in the period of Robert III, with a careless
Bridal of Polmood plot of wicked nobles, jealous
husbands, and ladies with too much spirit and time
on their hands. It is full of incongruities like a
shepherd who is also a "man of feeling"; Merlin and

his book of fate in red characters which blind the intruder (possibly anticipating Michael Scott of *The Three Perils of Man,* but sorely inappropriate here); echoes of Macbeth and Shakespearean language, such as "I'll do a deed/shall make the guileful heart of woman quake in future ages" and "Peace my heart! They come." But there are vivid passages, like that describing crazy Elenor, which is an attempt, albeit out of place, to describe mental breakdown.

What emerges clearly in this gallimaufry of magic and madness, Merlin and Macbeth, is that Hogg is obviously looking for a *form.* Long poems have failed him, since they limit his direct expression of all the folk lore and varying attitudes he wishes to take to it. Needing something looser, with a more natural language, he turns to poetic drama, but unfortunately lands on the form that reveals even greater incongruity, since the gap between Border shepherd and English Elizabethan is wider still than that between himself and the poetry of his age. *Sir Anthony Moore* (even his name should tell us!) is *Othello* set in sixteenth-century English, with a *Romeo and Juliet* ending, the heroine drinking her vial of poison like Juliet ("come Lethe, come/again I'll fill thy sleepy bowels up"). At this point one feels rather sad on Hogg's behalf, because there is no doubt he was misguidedly and zealously reading everything he thought would educate and improve him from Milton to Shakespeare, Ramsay to Wodrow. His *All-Hallow-Eve* is nevertheless a step forward in his development, for in addition to imitating much of the plot of Ramsay's *The Gentle Shepherd,* with the loves of Patie, Roger, Jennie and Peggie parallelled here with those of Gemel, Ben, Maldie and Gekan, there is exactly the same anti-romantic statement about marriage as Jennie uttered to Peggie. The warning is given to the girls that husbands "deface its [maidenhood's] fair and youthful bloom/and make a drudge o't." It is ironic indeed that Hogg, so good at capturing the realities of peasant life when he wishes, should here descend to imitating what *was* fresh a hundred years before in Ramsay, that willingness to celebrate the non-Arcadian side of shepherd life. The play does move Hogg nearer to the subject matter of *The Brownie of Bodsbeck,* though, with its apparent supernatural mystery which turns out, like the novel, to have a logical explanation, since a band of robbers are using the old witch as a "cover," just as the law-breaking covenanters of the novel use the supernatural figures of brownies to cover themselves. There is also some fine poetry in the witches' songs, comparable to those of the spirits in *The Three Perils of Man.* Both in this and Hogg's unfinished last play, written to fill the volume, *The Haunted Glen,* which is yet again as Hogg tells us based on "Tam Lin," there is very noticeably a great rise in the quality of the writing when the action deals with the material of "The Witch of Fife" and "Kilmeny." There is real fun, movement and beauty in this last, but it is the material either of poetry or of fiction, not drama. Hogg, on the evidence of *The Haunted Glen* was probably then working on *The Brownie of Bodsbeck* and *The Hunt of Eildon.* Presumably the return to the Borders in 1815 with the grant of a small farm in Yarrow had created a desire to return to the material of *The Mountain Bard.* Certainly the pre-occupation with poetry over the last fifteen years and more had been a costly diversion in terms of time (he was forty-eight when *The Brownie of Bodsbeck* came out) and effort, for the handful of really good poems it produced. Looking at the period overall, from the story poems of *The Mountain Bard* (and their lengthy anecdotal notes on wizards like Michael Scott and legends of Border warriors) to the fantastic journeys of *The Queen's Wake* and *The Pilgrims of the Sun,* it is obvious that Hogg was really looking for the right form in which to tell tales of the Borders. In the next six years, from 1818 to 1824, he was to make his greatest literary achievements in the forms most suited to his blend of earthly realism and fantastic imagination and ironic humour—that of the novel and short story.

NOTES

1. *Simpson,* p. 107.
2. *Autobiography,* p. 454.
3. Douglas Mack, *James Hogg: Selected Poems,* 1970, intro. p. xv.
4. *Works of the Ettrick Shepherd,* ed. Thomson, 1865, vol. II, p. 63.
5. *Works,* vol. II, p. 89.
6. *Simpson,* p. 57.
7. *Simpson,* p. 58.
8. David Daiches, *Robert Burns,* 1950, p. 38.
9. *Works,* vol. II, p. 62.
10. *Works,* vol. II, p. 86.
11. *Works,* vol. II, p. 95.
12. *Works,* vol. II, p. 97.
13. *Works,* vol. II, p. 64.
14. *Works,* vol. II, p. 65.
15. *Autobiography,* p. 465.
16. *Works,* vol. II, p. 72.
17. *Works,* vol. II, p. 73.
18. *Works,* vol. II, p. 73.
19. *Works,* vol. II, p. 72.
20. *Simpson,* p. 61.
21. *Simpson,* p. 73.

22. The later poetry and Hogg's songs generally are dealt with in Chapter Six.

23. David Daiches, *The Paradox of Scottish Culture*, p. 28.

24. *Works*, vol. II, p. 52.

25. *Mack*, p. xxi.

26. Scott persuaded Hogg that the old man should *not* be "burnit skin and bane," but to give the poem a happy ending should be rescued by his wife. *Domestic Manners*, p. 106.

27. *Works*, vol. II, p. 14.

28. *Simpson*, p. 70.

29. Alexander Scott, "Hogg's May of the Moril Glen," *Scottish Literary News*, vol. 3, no. 1, April 1973, pp. 9-16.

30. *Works*, vol. II, p. 100.

31. *Works*, vol. II, p. 100.

32. *Works*, vol. II, p. 102.

33. *Works*, vol. II, p. 103.

34. *Works*, vol. II, p. 103.

35. *Works*, vol. II, p. 174.

36. *Works*, vol. II, p. 174.

37. In addition to these supernatural poems, there are also poems like "The Powris of Moseke," comedies which are nevertheless in "The Witch of Fife" tradition.

38. *Works*, vol. II, p. 21.

39. *Works*, vol. II, p. 24.

40. *Works*, vol. II, pp. 24-25.

41. *Works*, vol. II, p. 393.

42. *Works*, vol. II, p. 386.

43. *Works*, vol. II, p. 323.

44. *Mack*, p. xxii.

45. John R. Mair, "A Note on Hogg's 'Kilmeny'," *Scottish Literary News*, vol. 3, no. 1, April 1973, pp. 17-21.

46. In a letter to William Blackwood, July 1829, quoted in the unpublished text of A. L. Strout, "Life and Letters of James Hogg, vol. II, p. 20 (In National Library of Scotland).

47. For Mary's unhappy reaction to impoverished Scotland, and Hogg's idealisation of the event, see *Simpson*, p. 83.

48. *Simpson*, p. 87.

49. *Autobiography*, p. 451.

50. *Works,* vol. II, p. 106. For the history of its composition, see *Autobiography,* p. 451.

51. *Works,* vol. II, p. 112.

52. The story can be read in *Scottish Short Stories 1800-1900,* ed. Douglas Gifford, 1971.

53. *Works,* vol. II, p. 119.

54. The version I quote is a blend of versions in F. J. Child, *English and Scottish Popular Ballads,* 1882-98; and G. Greig, *Last Leaves of Traditional Ballads,* 1925.

55. *Works,* vol. II, p. 120.

56 *Simpson,* p. 92.
Hogg had been reading John Wilson's "Isle of Palms"; "I was so greatly taken with many of his fanciful and visionary scenes, descriptive of bliss and woe, that it had a tendency to divest me occasionally of all worldly feelings." (*Autobiography,* p. 450). If Wilson was the worst of models for Hogg, it is perhaps also worth noting that William Tennant's mock-heroic description of the humours of the fair in James v's reign, with fairy sub-plots, had come out in 1812 and profoundly impressed Hogg (*Auster Fair*).

57. *Works,* vol. II, p. 163.

58. *Works,* vol. II, p. 166.

59. *Autobiography,* p. 448.

CHAPTER THREE

EARLY FICTION:
The Brownie of Bodsbeck (1818)
and *Basil Lee* (1820)

HOGG'S FIRST FICTION appeared in his magazine *The Spy*, which began in 1810 and lasted for only a year.[1] In a way which is reminiscent of Ramsay and Burns, he wrote in a dual *persona*. In one rôle he was the Spy, faking a background of gentle birth fallen on evil days, taking an observer's interest in psychological quirks, showing already his acute interest in morbid thought and action. Here also, however, was a fake point of view, which, in its attempt to be at one with polite Edinburgh, produced unconvincing stories of rakes' progresses and vices punished. But defiantly another *persona*, more closely related to the Ettrick Hogg, re-asserted itself as a more robust and honest teller of tales of country history, mystery, and the supernatural, who told in prose the tales based on the same material as used in *The Mountain Bard* and *The Queen's Wake*. A polarity had been established; insecurity about his social position had created a mild form of split creative personality. And here, hitherto unnoticed, lies one definite origin of that image of rustic naïveté and rough lyricism which was eventually to grow rank and disgusting to Hogg himself as the caricature shepherd of the *Noctes Ambrosianae*. One cannot divest Hogg of all blame in this. In the deliberate juxtaposition of the "posh" Spy and his restrained commentaries on drama with the awkward and simple utterances of John on the actors ("he has rather o'er mony capers and twirls wi' his fingers and

70

his cane; yon's scrimply natural . . ."[2]) Hogg himself means his audience to laugh at, as well as with, the clownish aspects of the peasant.

But nevertheless a significant step forward in Hogg's literary development had been taken, and that some four years before Scott's *Waverley* (1814). At least three strands of new effort in fiction can be seen, none destined in themselves for complete success, but together showing the range that Hogg had to bring together for *The Justified Sinner*. In *The Spy* Hogg separately and tentatively tried out stories of worthless anti-heroes, but psychologically interesting and autobiographically presented forerunners of Robert Wringhim and the Edinburgh Bailie; stories that presented the wealth of fairy lore and the range of supernatural figures of the Borders; and stories which are sensational and mysterious, their very effect depending on their lack of definite answers to their mysteries. The tale on "Instability in a Calling," a letter from a Berwickshire farmer, was to become the novel *Basil Lee*. This, with the unfinished "Love Adventures of George Cochrane," was the first step towards the recurrent Hogg anti-hero. The charming, gentle pastoral studies of children in the midst of the marvellous, "Duncan Campbell" and "The Country Laird," were to be revised as "The Woolgatherer." "The Ghost of Lochmaben" and "Love of Fame," with others, are tales of wraiths, sudden inexplicable disappearances which were to become as much as anything else the staple on which Hogg would always rely when long poems and novels had failed. These two stories and others were also to be revised, and along with the others would re-appear in *Winter Evening Tales* (1820), Hogg's only really successful collection of fiction.

But *The Spy* itself lasted only the year. It was considered too coarse. When girls were pregnant, Hogg said so directly. It contained a lot of earthy country situations, as well as sarcastic reflections on gentry—and this, amongst some of Hogg's best prose on country matters, a decidedly unromantic account of a trip to the Highlands,[3] as well as some hackneyed "moralistic" writing, is all that can be found to account for the desertion of Hogg's generally deserving magazine by his subscribers. He said later that he saw his mistake.

> I despised the fastidiousness and affectation of the people . . . the literary ladies in particular agreed . . . that I would never write a sentence which deserved to be read.[4]

And in the final number of *The Spy* he wrote that

> The learned, the enlightened, and polite circles of this flourishing metropolis disdained either to be amused or instructed by the ebullitions of humble genius. Enemies, swelling with the most rancorous spite, grunted in every corner . . . Pretended friends . . . liberal in their advices . . . took every method in their power to lessen the work in the esteem of others by branding its author with designs the most subversive of all civility and decorum. . . .[5]

Thus from the beginning of his fiction criticism was to inhibit his full-blooded response to life. Already critics had adopted an attitude to Hogg which accepted his pleasant country songs, his moments of poetic genius, his sketches of the shepherd's life, but advised him not to attempt more.

But Hogg was resilient in these early years in Edinburgh. He decided not to give in to the literary ladies and sensitive gentlemen, and between 1810 and 1820 added to and amended the early *Spy* stories for his collection *Winter Evening Tales,* most noticeably in deepening and tautening the sense of horrific mystery in stories like "Adam Bell" and "The Long Pack." This development came to fruition in the novel *The Brownie of Bodsbeck,* which although published in 1818 and thus before *Winter Evening Tales* in fact post-dates most of the material in the latter. Hogg also increased the element of Border lore and supernatural in stories like "The Woolgatherer" by interpolating more varied and colourful creatures like bogles, kelpies and other agents of the "other landscape" than the straightforward wraiths and apparitions of *The Spy* stories. *The Hunt of Eildon,* published with "The Woolgatherer" and *The Brownie of Bodsbeck,* was the biggest step forward in this area towards *The Three Perils of Man,* the masterpiece in the kind. And lastly —although of course all these aspects interplay to a certain extent—Hogg continually deepened his interest in the anti-hero and morbid psychology, unsuccessfully in this period in the short novel *The Bridal of Polmood* in *Winter Evening Tales,* but with real comic and satiric success in another short novel in the same collection called *Basil Lee.* These three areas of fiction, within this period of development, will now be considered, with an analysis of the major achievement in each.

It is a long way from the crude sensationalism of dismembered corpses falling out of the sky in "The Dreadful Story of McPherson" and the heavy-handed explanations given for Adam Bell's mysterious disappearance in "The Love of Fame," to the revision of the latter into the tauter, open-endedly mysterious and possibly supernatural tale "Adam Bell" and the dramatically presented, compelling riddles of *The Brownie of Bodsbeck*. No single short story illustrates the improvement better than "The Long Pack" (1817), a story so popular in the Borders that it appeared in several chapbook editions over many years. It begins with simple mystery of the earlier kind. A packman arrives at a country house with the longest, broadest, thickest pack ever seen. He asks to leave it with the skeleton staff of old man, boy and maid—and from then on it fascinates them in an uncanny way, till, Alice being horrified at seeing it moving, young Edward discharges his ancient gun into it, with blood and groans as the result! So far the tale is straightforward, but then follows a further mystery, superbly evoked, with attention to convincing detail in a way which Defoe and Swift would have appreciated, as Hogg describes the "artful and curious" way a man is packed inside, and raises a deeper mystery. Why does the dead man, quite apart from being inside at all, possess cutlass, pistols and silver windcall? The concrete detail balances the mounting mystery perfectly. The pace is balanced, till "an hour past midnight" Edward blows the whistle—and a strange body of men appear, to be ambushed. But only in the morning do the inmates of the house venture out, to find, in the growing dawn, "that the corpses were removed, and nothing left but large sheets of frozen blood."[6] The mystery of the pack has given way to a much deeper and ultimately inexplicable mystery, and one which will recur again in Hogg in tales from *The Justified Sinner* to "The Baron St. Gio" and "John Lochy," of dark forces, possibly supernatural or merely great earthly conspiracies, surrounding innocents who see only the parts of the web about them. The Long Pack riddle is never answered—though sundry great men's sons are missing in the district, and the packman's grave robbed of his corpse.

Here Hogg tentatively tries a device which will become the trademark of his greatest tales. Ambiguity, creative and unresolved, will become the essence of his mysteries, and place the best on a par with stories like Hawthorne's "Young Goodman Brown" or James's "The Turn of the Screw," which use the same method of presenting the reader with a final dualism of interpretation. It is thus all the more interesting to find that his best "mystery" novel of this period, *The Brownie of Bodsbeck,* was only at the last moment given an ending which resolved what had been hitherto a supernatural/rational ambiguity.

But this is a major achievement, and deserves attention in itself. It is not, however much Hogg may have been influenced at the outset by Scott's *Old Mortality* (1816), historical romance, despite Scott-like addition of historical background material in later editions. The book opens with the terse statement of two riddles. Why does Wat of Chapelhope, a sturdy, sensible Border shepherd-farmer, come off the hills saying "It will be a bloody night in Gemsop, this."? Why is he hungry, since he took enough food for six to the hills? And more riddles soon follow. What is wrong with his daughter Katharine, who is behaving most strangely, especially at night? What exactly has been seen by the herdman?

On Monanday night he cam yont to stop the ewes aff the hogg-fence, but or it was lang he saw a white thing an' a black thing comin' up the Houm close thegither; they cam' by within three catloups of him—he grippit his cudgel firm, and was aince gaun to gie them strength o' airm, but his power failed him, and a' his sinnens grew like dockens; there was a kind o' glamour came o'er his e'en too, for a' the Hope an' the heaven grew as derk as tar an' pitch —but the setting moon shone even in their faces, and he saw them as weel as it had been fore-day. The tane was a wee bit hurklin' crile of an unearthly thing, as shrinkit an' wan as he had lien seven years in the grave; the tither was like a young woman—an' what d'ye think? He says he'll gang to death wi't that it was outher our dochter or her wraith.[7]

This dramatic, direct entry to the events is typical of the story, as is the superb use of dialect in a way which not even Scott or Galt can better. Only after these vivid first scenes does Hogg explain some background. We learn of the atrocities of a diabolic Claverhouse, determined "utterly to extirpate the seed of the whining psalm-singing race from the face of the earth," but described hardly in Scott's objective, historical manner. But before we tire of this Hogg returns to Wat and his own racy account of what happened when he, no devout churchgoer, met the Covenanters hiding in the rain in the hills. What a superb extended dramatic monologue this is! And over and above the use of Scots which is as fitting in its revelation of Wat's character and as vivid for dramatic narrative as that of "Holy Willie's Prayer," "Wandering Willie's Tale" from *Redgauntlet* (1824) or "Tod Lapraik" in *Catriona* (1893) is the magnificent way that the character revealed, Wat's generous and impulsive humanity, contrasts so starkly with the "haggard severity" and passionate Presbyterianism of the Covenanters. Here, for the first time in Hogg, is that mature traditional peasant healthiness of attitude which Hogg will so sharply contrast with fanaticism in the juxtaposition of the Laird of Dalcastle and his son George with the Reverend Wringhim and his son Robert in *The Justified Sinner,* Scottish integrity set formally against Scottish sickness. And yet the Covenanters are not satirised emotively. Indeed, their cheerful courage, their tough resilience *is* more convincing than the selfish fanaticism of Scott's Habbakuk Mucklewrath, and there is a powerful sense that their political "sins" are really justified.

> I had two brave and beautiful sons, and I had but two; one of these had his brains shot out on the moss of Monyhive without a question, charge, or reply. I gathered up his brains and shattered skull with these hands, tied them in my own napkin, and buried him alone . . . his murderers stood by and mocked me. . . . Should ever the murderer Clavers, or any of his hellhounds of the north, dare set foot in heaven, one look from the calm benignant face of my martyred son would drive them out howling! [8]

Broadly speaking, the two characters Wat and Katharine, and the riddles attaching to each, give the novel its form, whereby Wat, with the "open-air" Covenanting action, dominates the first half. Lurking below this straightforward story of Claverhouse's atrocities and Wat's aid to the persecuted, is the darker mystery of the supernatural Brownie, and its strange relation with Katharine. In a way this structure anticipates that of *The Justified Sinner*, with its more straightforward, objective first part, followed by the stranger, deeper Sinner's account. Wat is a bluff, open nature, and it is fitting we should be introduced to the strangeness through his pragmatic and sane view of events. Like Blanchard, the good minister of *The*

Justified Sinner, Wat is a yardstick of sound, instinctive moral sense. On this base Hogg can build some weird but credible developments, like the suspicions that Katharine may be a witch, with even her mother so terrified that she hints at burning her, or the strange, Meg Merrilees-like figure of Nannie Elshinder, the only family servant who remains, who mumbles apparent madness but has disturbing moments of lucid relevance, or animals in terror at inexplicable noises from the haunted Old Room in Wat's house. But most taxing so far of our credulity is the first really incongruous episode, concerning Young Kennedy, who falls into strange company on the moors,

> a multitude of hideous beings, with green clothes, and blue faces, who sat in a circle round a small golden bump . . .[9]

who carry him off a great distance but return him (after he says the name of Jesus three times) half-mad, in a coffin, to Chapelhope.

This is too much for an already overstrained narrative to sustain. As happens so often with Hogg, he lacks the overall controlling sense to see the inappropriateness of what is indeed a colourful episode. With this sheer excess of diablerie he pushes his covenanting novel too far towards the comic supernatural of *The Three Perils of Man,* towards a different idiom and tradition. This and the story of Jasper the shepherd boy and his knitting are simply out of place.

The rest of the first part is good. The sadistic, mocking interrogation of Wat's family and servants is both nauseating and comic, a real achievement, as peasant shrewdness talks its way out of desperate danger. The only jarring note here is possibly when

Hogg goes too far in reducing Claverhouse. He makes him not only a diabolic persecutor, but a sly interferer with maidens, who is manhandled by Wat in a way that leaves him little dignity when Wat catches him accosting his daughter. This is a pity, since Hogg had established a powerful and sustained devil metaphor in regard to Claverhouse which gives him, apart from this petty scene, a kind of epic malevolent force. Certainly one understands why Walter Scott did not like the depiction!

The height of the drama of this first half is reached in the description of the atrocities against children. The novel takes on an almost documentary realism, and the events are told with such spare and convincing detail that one is convinced that here Hogg works very close to tradition, and the passages still evoke angered participation from the reader.[10] Hogg's personal addition here to the traditional account would seem to be the honest, kindly Highlander, McPherson, who refuses to be part of the killing:

> Hersel would be fighting the Campbells, sword in hand, for every inch of the Moor of Rannoch; but she does not like to be pluffing and shooting through te bodies of te poor helpless isignificant crheatures. . . . Now, Cot t-n sh-, sh-, she'll rather be fighting Clavers and all her dragoons, pe-pefore she'll be killing tat dear good lhad.[11]

This is the old device of contrasting the sane man with the unnatural events that Hogg uses so well, but it is also clever plotting, since the same McPherson will take a great liking to Wat when he is sent prisoner to Edinburgh to be tried before the Privy Council, and will be (with great irony and comedy) the means of Wat's triumph at the eleventh hour.

With Wat off to Edinburgh as prisoner for helping Covenanters, the attention focuses on Katharine. For a time the change is for the bad, for she is artificial, cool, talks flawless and lifeless English, is too perfect; and the digressive material increases, as does the incongruous, crude clowning. The picture of the hypocritical spy curate Clerk who wants to wrestle all night privately with Katharine for her soul may be an anticipation of Wringhim senior's similar situation with Lady Dalcastle in *The Justified Sinner,* but it lacks specific ironic relevance here and is too much mere sexual insinuation for its own irrelevant sake, like the minister with Sally in *The Three Perils of Women.*

Katharine and the Brownie are still unknown quantities to us. Hogg handles this wonderful situation well, especially when faced with the challenge of actually showing his Brownie.

> A being of such unearthly dimensions entered, as no pen may ever wholly define. It was the Brownie of Bodsbeck . . . small of stature, and its whole form utterly misshaped . . . its look, and every lineament of its face, were indicative of agony—its locks were thin, dishevelled and white, and its back hunched up behind its head. There seemed to be more of the same species of haggard beings lingering behind the door. . . .[12]

And there is a stroke of genius worthy of the Hawthorne of "Goodman Brown" in the handling of the curate's attempted seduction. On the entry of the Brownie, he faints, is removed, and wakens next morning. He knocks at Katharine's door, to find her "in her usual neat and cleanly morning dress. He stared in her face . . . it was a face of calm, decent

serenity, and wore no shade of either shame or anger."
No one described like this, of course, can be a witch.
But what explanation else? How do we account for
the fate of Clerk, who is carried off in a coffin, not to
be seen for years, after the Brownie has strangely
reproached him for his hypocrisy and licentiousness?

It is fascinating that Hogg contemplated leaving these
questions unanswered by a last chaper. Would the
story have "resonated," like *The Justified Sinner*,
between the rational explanation and the supernatural
possibility? As it is, the eleventh-hour explanation
that the Brownies are Covenanters hiding in wet caves
(hence their deformity) who come out at dark, that
Katharine has been helping them, that Nannie is the
grief-crazed wife of the Brownie himself, John Brown,
their leader, immediately prohibits the dual response
the story *might* have had.

There are two last striking features of the novel.
The first is the extremely entertaining, but most
obvious digression in the novel, the prayers of the
bewildered peasants, led by Davie Tait.[13] These really
belong with other peasant studies like "Storms" or
"The Shepherd's Dog." They are vivid anecdotes full
of fun, but pulled in by the hair of the head at this point
in the novel. Technically they can be justified as
showing humble people's response to the horrors about
them, and they are acute cameos of the paradoxically
narrow yet colourful nature of peasant imagination.
But compared to the magnificent comic ending to the
perils of Wat in Edinburgh they can clearly be seen
as basically irrelevant.

Hogg's genius is at its height in the courtroom
scenes, Wat's fervent, rich dialect contrasting with
the cold standard English of prosecution and defence.
But it is the central irony which he contrives which

raises this to the level of his finest work. For, on McPherson's advice, Wat, nearing a black end to his "rigged" trial, blows up in a manner that clears him of all suspicion of being one of the faithful.

> But now, thinks I to mysel, things canna be muckle waur wi' me; the scrows come fairly to the neb o' the miresnipe now . . . sae I musters up a' my wrath up into my face, and when the judge . . . put the question again, I never heedit what it was, but set up my birses an' spak to them as they had been my herd callants. "What the de'il are ye a' after?" quoth I. "Curse the hale pack o' ye, do ye think that auld Wat Laidlaw's a Whig, or wad do aught against his king, or the laws o' his country? . . . had I ony twa o' ye on Chapelhope-flow thegither, I wad let ye find strength o' airm for aince." Here the wily chap Geordie Lockie [the prosecution] stappit me in great agitation, and beggit me to keep my temper and answer his Lordship. . . .[14]

As Wat damns them all, the court starts clapping; then ensues a "wee quiet" while the men of power "speak across" to one another. Hogg is always good at courtroom scenes, but never better; this, in its ironic inferences as to the expediency of law, in its evocation of atmosphere, is as good as the comparable scenes in *The Heart of Midlothian* (1818). And Wat's final wry musing encapsulates the absurdity of the political situation that lies behind the trial. Wat is judged a worthy man (indeed!)—

> I thankit his Lordship; but thinks I to mysel, ye're a wheen queer chaps! Ye shoot fock for prayin' an' reading the bible, an' whan ane curses an' damns

ye, ye ca' him a true honest man! I wish ye be nae the deil's bairns, the hale wort o' ye! [15]

As long as Hogg works with such objectively *real* Border material, types like Charlie Scott of Yardbire in *The Three Perils of Man*, or Dick Rickleton of *The Three Perils of Women* or the Laird in *The Justified Sinner* he cannot go far wrong. (It is thus doubly fascinating that his other highly successful type should be the very subjective, morbid and unhealthy anti-hero). Wat has an important place in the development of Scottish fiction. He represents an older, valid set of traditional Scottish values, together with integration of mind, which will increasingly be absent from the major Scottish fiction of the nineteenth century. If one compares him as a hero with Scott's Edward Waverley, or even Henry Morton in *Old Mortality*, with Walkinshaw in Galt's *Entail* (1823), with the morbid or one-sided or diseased epic figures of Stevenson and Douglas Brown, then his *wholeness* of head and heart, optimism and pragmatism, is at once outstanding. Only Hogg, with his roots deep in an older Scotland, could present such a type at the centre of his novel. Even in Scott's hands, such convincing peasant figures are relegated, like Dandie Dinmont, or even more significantly, Edie Ochiltree, to the past and the minor rôles.

There is one last interesting aspect of *The Brownie of Bodsbeck,* and that is the technical. However confused the novel sometimes becomes, there is no denying that Hogg's *aim* was to present his material in a novel, direct and indeed experimental way. Look at the way the novel opens, with its (not entirely successful) attempt to suggest immediacy, by that arresting opening, by the continual breaking off to what's happening simultaneously elsewhere. It is, in admittedly the crudest of forms, an attempt like that of Conrad in *Nostromo,* to show a large set of bewildering events through a series of different, contemporaneous flashback and contrasting scenes. It doesn't entirely work, but is it not fascinating that a self-taught shepherd writer should be trying out such techniques of storytelling? At the very least, should he not have been encouraged, involved as an equal in discussion, by his peers like Scott, Wilson and Lockhart? The novel is at least as good as Galt's treatment of the same topic, *Ringan Gilhaize* (1823), and better by far than applauded romances like Thomas Dick Lauder's *The Wolf of Badenoch* (1827). It is no *Old Mortality,* but it has strengths and a richness which that novel lacks, and is better than much of Scott's second-rate work like *The Monastery* (1820). But Scott's attitude speaks worlds in his letter to Laidlaw at the time, when, referring to *The Brownie of Bodsbeck* and its companion pieces, *The Hunt of Eildon* and "The Woolgatherer," he says, "The cubs have not succeeded well . . . but they are sadly vulgar, to be sure."[16]

The revision of the *Spy* story "The Country Laird" to "The Woolgatherer" shows that, along with Hogg's refinement of his sense of the mysterious, he increasingly wanted to explore, beyond wraiths and apparitions, the world of devils, fairies, bogles and brownies for whom his shepherd Barnaby had sketched out the "groundrules" (quoted above, p. 19). This is Hogg's first statement in fiction of what is to be a major feature of his work until repeated criticism disheartened him. The modern reader will, however, have none of Scott and Wilson's dislike for the multiplicity of creatures and the vivid, often hauntingly beautiful scenes that make up this world, so different, so much richer in range and colour, and so much more authentic in their being the organic culture of an ancient way of life compared to the thinner, contrived omens and mysticism of Galt's *The Omen* (1825) and *The Entail* (1823), or the machinery of astrology in *Guy Mannering* (1815), let alone the whole range of synthetic supernatural from Lewis's *The Monk* (1796) to Maturin's *Melmoth the Wanderer* (1820). Hogg's tales of this world are *not* "confused magic," but descendants of an age-old mythology with its own logic and its own organic laws. "The Woolgatherer" became a loose assembly of short tales of the kind, but its companion piece, the long-short story *The Hunt of Eildon,* significantly increased his range. For the first time Hogg went back to the middle ages; not as far as in *The Three Perils of Man,* but to James IV, although in both works the "history" is really folk-history, a welter of popular memories, often confused, and conflating deeds of different kings and heroes.

> The King had betted with the Earl of Hume and Lord Belhaven, seven steers, seven palfreys, seven deer greyhounds, and seven gold rings, that his two snow-white hounds, Mooly and Scratch, would kill a roe-deer started on any part of the Eildon hills. . . . [17]

This is the initial wager/condition common to the Ballads and *The Three Perils of Man,* with the ritual numbers and ingredients which medieval listeners loved to hear repeated. The two hounds are lost sisters, Elen and Clare of Rosaline, transformed to protect the King. With something of the Gothic and artificial in their well-spoken melodramatic ways, nevertheless there is real Kilmeny-like beauty in Hogg's handling of the ancient legend. And for the first time in a tale, we have the Devil himself, opposed to these curiously pagan-Christian virtuous ladies in white who become white hounds, as an old gruff knight who is eventually discovered and expelled in flame through the use of holy water. While hardly presented with the ambiguity or irony of *The Justified Sinner,* nevertheless in the *pattern* of hints and clues behind the narrative as to which forces are good and which bad, with the reader eventually coming to "sense" the truth through the reactions of animals or the use of a colour-system, there is something of the elaborate, game-like richness of the later great novels. There is also the disturbing atmosphere of the curious love-hate relationship which exists between Devil and victim in *The Justified Sinner* and so many of the later great short stories like "The Brownie of the Black Haggs" and "The Baron St. Gio," and expressed in equally disturbing images. The two hounds pursue Evil in one of its many forms, that of

a bonny, braw, young lady, a' clad in white, about a hunder paces frae me, an' she was aye looking back an' running as gin she wantit to be at the Eildon Tree . . . they soon o'ertook her, threw her down, an' tore her, an' worried her; an' I heard her makin' a noise as gin she had been laughin' ae while an singin' another, an' O I thought her sang was sweet. . . .[18]

But Hogg does not sustain this high level of treatment. Just as in his poetry and drama of the years immediately before this he had failed to fuse his various kinds of inspiration, so now he introduces incongruity and jarring burlesque into the tale. Croudy the shepherd and the comedy of his wooings has some fun and vitality to offer, but the transitions between levels in this story are awkwardly managed, and when the two sisters change Croudy into a boar, the effect is similar to the putting of a false nose on the Queen of the Fairies. Once in either world of faery or burlesque, though, the involvement is complete. The challenge for Hogg as an artist is obviously to *fuse* these two worlds. Later he will succeed, but even now the tale is enjoyable for its lively parts, its Dunbar-like comic riots, its swift changes of mood and scene. And in certain scenes, like the genuinely moving expression of the dog's love for his metamorphosed master, with the ludicrous and the pathetic rubbing shoulders in the form of collie and boar, one can see that Hogg is developing the use of humour as a means of resolving his two worlds of the medieval and the modern. Here, in the witchcraft scenes, or when the lovers are turned into moorfowl, the improbable and fantastic is softened and humanised through the use of a boisterous, ironic or simply good-humoured and whimsical tone.

One last characteristic of *The Hunt of Eildon* had appeared in *The Brownie of Bodsbeck* in slighter form, and appears used to great ironic effect in *Basil Lee* and the major fiction. It is the way in which Hogg's idiom *reduces* the pompous and powerful in favour of the peasant and the simply good-hearted. Claverhouse had been treated this way; and James iv is treated likewise. Out of this peasant and reductive idiom Hogg's later and greater, genuine ironic and anti-chivalrous vision of *The Three Perils of Man* will grow, though at the moment the weakness of the view is more apparent, as it on the one hand shows James to be a witch-burner and superstitious, unstable monarch, and yet on the other *justifies* his destruction of twelve witches at Leader, "after which act of duty his conscience became a good deal lightened."[19]

But *The Hunt of Eildon* is an important example of Hogg's development in his supernatural and legendary vein. It is highly significant that, just as with *The Three Perils of Man,* when in later years Hogg had been demoralised by repeated criticism or just plain neglect, so that he turned against his own love of this "other world" fiction, he cut out of this story a long Tam Lin-like ballad, and apologised or excused the tale in a footnote to make it more acceptable to nineteenth-century readers:

> From several parts of this traditionary tale it would appear, that it is a floating fragment of some ancient allegorical romance, the drift of which it is not easy to comprehend.[20]

Muddled the tale may be; but it angers the modern critic to find a writer of such genius being forced through his critical mis-reception into such an embarrassing dissociation of himself from his own offspring. It is to Scott's discredit that he led such criticism, calling the tale "the most ridiculous story" he had ever read.[21]

In this arbitrary, but, one hopes, not irrelevant separation of Hogg's development into three strands it must be realised that often they overlap. For example, "The Woolgatherer" is not just a story characterised by Hogg's love of the legendary and marvellous. It is also a story about a "missing heir," with much of Hogg's love of mystery. Similarly, *The Brownie of Bodsbeck* has within it episodes more wonderful than mysterious, while *Basil Lee,* the best example of the third strand, the love of the anti-heroic, inglorious protagonist, has many scenes of the supernatural.

Nevertheless, I feel that one can see Hogg as moving forward in this period with three fronts, three "prongs" to his inspiration. The third is most bizarre and intriguing.

It is paradoxical that a man so rooted in the timeless past of the countryside should have been so fascinated by morbid behaviour and the details of warped psychology. George Kitchin has pointed out that a characteristic of Edinburgh fiction of the period was that it took such an interest,[22] and it is true that novels like *Waverley, Adam Blair* (1822), *Mathew Wald* (1824), *The Entail, The Provost* (1822) and characters like Balfour of Burleigh and Redgauntlet establish a peculiarly Scottish intensity of interest in the workings of powerful minds under extreme pressure. But whatever the Edinburgh interest of the time, I think it can be shown that Hogg's interest in this area is not inherited from these novelists, but can be seen in his very earliest prose. Compare the Spy's account of his "modus operandi" with Gilmartin's in *The Justified Sinner*; the first in 1810, the second in 1824.

I am now become an observer so accurate, that by contemplating a person's features minutely, modelling my own after the same manner as nearly as possible, and putting my body into the same posture . . . I can ascertain the compass of their minds and thoughts . . . the way that they *would* think about anything. . . .[23]

If I contemplate a man's features seriously, mine own gradually assume the very same appearance and character. And . . . more, by contemplating a face minutely, I not only attain the same likeness . . . but . . . I attain the very same ideas as well as the same mode of arranging them.[24]

The rôle of the Spy is important not just in Hogg's magazine but throughout all his fiction. From the very beginning the emphasis on the importance of "observation" and "contemplation" in essay and story isolates a major characteristic of Hogg's which was to manifest itself in two complementary ways, and produce two kinds of fiction which persisted till Hogg died.

One is seen in the Spy's fascination for the results in action of mental disturbance and stress, and for quirks of character notably out of the usual. For example, *Basil Lee* began as a study of instability of mind leading almost to self-destruction. The first version of "Adam Bell" was based on contemplation of the "Love of Fame," "as this passion operates upon the human mind." But most important in the study of this trait in Hogg's work is the article called "Impatience Under Misfortunes."[25] It examines several "case-histories" of different ways of exhibiting stress, like a negro's reaction to Home's tragedy *Douglas;* an idiot's reaction to the death of a dog; or a girl's inappropriate, weird laughter at misfortune. Hogg is not being melodramatic in these sketches, but has a genuine interest in the *real* person, like "the Knight":

In the event of any cross accident, or vexatious incident happening to him, he makes straight towards his easy chair—sits calmly down upon it—clenches his right hand, with the exception of his forefinger, which is suffered to continue straight—strikes his fist violently against his left shoulder—keeps it in that position, with his eyes fixed on one particular point, till he has cursed the event and all connected with it most heartily,—then with a countenance of perfect good humour, he indulges in a pleasant laugh.[26]

These slighter sketches will be revised into the deeper study of *The Shepherd's Calendar* (1829), but they are the basis of important trial efforts in dramas of this period like *The Profligate Princes,* otherwise unsuccessful short stories like "Welldean Hall," and a novel Hogg valued out of all proportion to its real worth, published in the *Winter Evening Tales* as *The Bridal of Polmood*.[27]

This was universally condemned as bad historical romance in Scott's manner, but in fact it is no such thing. The "history" here is mere *papier-mâché* folk memory as background for a study of psychological stress set up in a triangle of love, with Hogg's first attempt to describe a murderous lunatic, whose love was "rather like a frenzy of the mind than a passion founded on esteem," the jealous forester Polmood. Hogg also works sincerely and sometimes with real insight in his study of Polmood's wilful, lively wife, Elizabeth. She may exasperate and strain our credulity, but she is never dull. Nor are the superb Games before the king, when Polmood exhibits maniacal strength against his rivals. Every win of Polmood or his rival Carmichael is designed to build up Polmood's violent jealousy and Carmichael's hate, with a tautness and necessity of connection between event and emotion which will be so much more effective in *The Justified Sinner*. But there is real psychological truth amongst the flaws, together with a spasmodic but genuine theme of anti-romance and irony at the expense of courtly and chivalrous pretensions.

But there is one fault that stands out which was the bane of Hog's poetry and continued to blight much of his fiction till he died. It is that tendency to lapse into the inappropriate and incongruous with no warning whatsoever which marred *The Hunt of Eildon,* and here shows itself in the extended "mistakes of a night" horseplay of the King and his nobles as they jink in and out of assorted ladies' bedrooms. Much of the real intensity is dissipated immediately, never to be regained, so that we are left with a novel zig-zagging unpredictably between scenes of insane jealousy and scenes of horseplay in high places. The gap between these illustrates perfectly the split basic to Hogg's creative personality, between the peasant and the man of letters. The story also demonstrates a point vital to a real understanding of Hogg's genius. Edith Batho attacked it thus:

> As Hogg knew nothing of courts or of the sixteenth century the result of his combined ignorance and boldness is a story madder than most.[28]

But, as *The Three Perils of Man* shows, Hogg's lack of *historical* knowledge or of aristocracy need not prevent success, but the essential factor in that case is that he must have a unified point of view, a consistency of attitude behind his imagined world. *The Three Perils of Man* has such a view, the racy, ironic and reductive peasant's-eye-view of kings and chivalry, which renders its improbabilities and zany events totally acceptable, whereas *The Bridal* lacks this vital, whole creative consciousness, and like so many other examples in Hogg's dramas, his long poem *Mador of the Moor,* his "Welldean Hall," or outstandingly his *Three Perils of Women,* the result is fragmentation into jarring themes, tones and effects. The surprising thing is that Hogg often produces his failures of fragmented vision almost at the same time as his marvellous successes—as is the case with the outstanding short novel of this period, *Basil Lee.*

We have been examining Hogg's interest in the observation of morbid psychology, and I argued that there were two complementary ways he developed this. One was to depict the workings of passion *objectively,* as in Polmood the lunatic. The other reveals itself in *Basil Lee* and "The Love Adventures of George Cochrane," the lesser of the two, but of secondary interest here to *Basil* for the fact that it is also presented from the autobiographical point of view of the anti-hero. In both there is still the interest in warped psychology, not on the gothic and romantic scale of Polmood, but on the more mundane and, to Hogg, more familiar level of peasants (or slightly above) with roots in Scottish society, acting and speaking in a way Hogg really knows, presented *subjectively.*

The Justified Sinner fuses both of these interests, but *Basil Lee* is still a major achievement in the form of the dramatic monologue of a selfish ne'er-do-weel, told with immense gusto *and,* for the first time, a unifying anti-romantic attitude which deliberately sets out to defy both the conventions of polite society and of the novel itself at that time. Almost certainly this is due to Hogg's resilient, independence of spirit reasserting itself, for the story is that very tale which in *The Spy* offended Edinburgh taste with its blunt pregnancies, so that Hogg is now cocking a snook at his blue-stocking critics by *developing* the tale for *Winter Evening Tales.*

It is true, probably because it is a "trial run" in the same field, that *Basil Lee* lacks *The Justified Sinner*'s taut structure. It is in four parts which often strain its unity. First we witness Basil's instability in whatever job he takes up, from shepherd to grocer to farmer to soldier, then he goes to Canada, where he meets the prostitute Clifford and his strange, diabolic enemy who seems tied to his fortunes, Lieutenant Colin Frazer. The third part is Basil's vastly amusing account of his cowardly participation in the American Wars of Independence, while the fourth, the most digressive, brings him home by way of shipwreck and Lewis, to Edinburgh and a real ironic twist in conclusion.

The content and the form are for the first time in Hogg absolutely at one, probably because the subjective presentation allows (apart from the Lewis episodes, which lose the character of Basil in their telling) the peripatetic, self-indulgent material. But Basil is also an ironic device, powerfully used to mock many aspects of genteel convention. For example, Basil, trying out being a shepherd,

> entered upon this celebrated classical employment with raptures of delight. . . . I rejoiced in the opportunity of reading so many delightful books, learning so many fine songs . . . and above all, of taking Jessy below my plaid . . .[29]

but when he does, he gets bored with reading, no one listens to his songs and whatever he did with Jessie, "it seems this had been a freedom of which the little minx did not approve; for thenceforward a ragamuffin . . . was sent with my meat." His very dog seems selfish to him, and leaves, while the early rising, the wet clothes, the sheep-smearing with tar, all lead him to conclude that

> the life of a shepherd, instead of being the most delightful and romantic, was the most dull and wretched state of existence.[30]

This, from their Shepherd, was a new picture, less sublime than Edinburgh was used to. The ironic attitude is sustained throughout, with real comedy, as when Grocer Lee sells vitriol by mistake as a dram to a highland drover, or Farmer Lee finds out that his ideal way of life is a myth, and that the countryside is laughing at his brisk gallopings and self-importance, culminating in his being turfed into the quagmire at the foot of a dunghill by a gypsy, and his housekeeper getting pregnant. Basil turns all polite customs of love upside down, and with a candour reminiscent of Defoe's Moll Flanders or Boswell's *London Journal* admits all.

> Jessie . . . had lately been married, which I did not strive much to prevent, having laid a plan with myself of seducing her affections afterwards. No sooner was the ceremony over, than I set about my laudable schemes . . . but the little devil thought proper to inform her husband, and not being aware of this on my return, I had nearly paid very dear. . . .[31]

This is the tone of *Basil Lee* in a nutshell, and is quite deliberate in its inversion of polite values. Funniest and most pointed of these deliberate mockeries of social types is Hogg's picture of Basil as soldier-hero, which is uncannily close to the anti-heroic adventures of the modern *Flashman* series of George Macdonald Fraser. Bearing in mind the chivalrous soldiers of Scott and Thomas Dick Lauder, a norm which obtained in Scottish fiction down through the work of James Grant and Whyte-Melville to Crockett and Neil Munro, it is all the more marvellous that Basil is such a completely realised and convincing rogue and coward. In sailing to Canada, he meets his arch-enemy Frazer, and ultimately is challenged to a duel. Hogg's evocation of his wriggling cowardice makes the reader squirm, as first Basil pretends religious principles prevent it; then argues humanity:

> For God's sake . . , I will rather make any acknowledgement he likes, than kill the honest brave fellow, and have his blood on my head . . .[32]

Basil's visions of mutilation, his willingness to crawl (literally) raise the embarrassment to a pitch which culminates in Basil's final hypocrisy.

> Frazer . . . held out his (hand) in the most proud disdainful way, while I with great bluntness took hold of it, and gave it a hearty squeeze and a shake. "Captain, man," says I—and I fear the tear was standing in my eye—"Captain, man, I little thought it would ever come to this with us! "
> "You did not, did you," replied he, "and fat te deil did you pe taking her to pe?" and with that he flung my hand away.[33]

And in keeping with Basil's meanness of spirit, he fights at his enemy's eyes, trying to prick them, and by accident wounds him and wins the duel by "sticking my sword directly in a part of his body which I do not choose to name."

The quarrel has been over a girl, Clifford, who in many ways is the finest achievement in the story, as she is both heroine, in the fullest sense of possessing dignity and charity and selfless love for Basil—and an Inverness prostitute. This mocks all conventional fiction of the time, but is all the more effective for not being a caricature, but a warm, convincing picture which throws what Hogg sees as polite and hypocritical standards back in the teeth of the critics who

96

had censured the original story. And Basil is never more sordid than in his dealings with this unconventional and angelic whore, as he changes his stance towards her, sometimes congratulating himself on his goodness, sometimes despising her but unable to break, till, having won false glory in duel and war:

> I thought is was base that there was no one to enjoy the emoluments and pride of my growing rank, but the daughter of a despicable highland cooper—a wench brought up among girds and shavings, or perhaps in a herring barrel.[34]

It is not her prostitution—that can be hidden—but her class that Basil now objects to. She, with dignity, anticipates his intention, and leaves him—which, of course, and convincingly, turns his scorn to infatuation.

But the high point of the story is the American Campaign. Despite all his cowardice, abandoning the colours, trying to flee, he gets tangled up with a Yankee dragoon who is wounded, and fearing for his life even from him, Basil kills both horse and dragoon. When the confusion clears, he is bathed in blood, has instinctively grabbed the colours, and is greeted by an English officer:

> "Well done, young Scot," cried he, and shook me by the hand; "By G—, sir, I say well done! You have behaved like a hero!" "The devil I have," thought I... [and, delirious with fear] ... seized the long bloody halberd once more, and with my eyes gleaming madness and rage, and, as I was told, with my teeth clenched, and grinning like a mad dog, I rushed on in the front... wounded every man that came within my reach, pricking them

always in the face, about the eyes and nose, which they could not stand. . . ."[35]

In this carrying of the anti-hero as far against convention as can be without once losing credibility lies Hogg's superb success. Basil here may be despicable, but elsewhere Hogg balances this by portraying his sensitivity, albeit warped, his fear, his loneliness. There is a sense of reality about his actions which is absent in much of the successful fiction of the time. One need only compare this with John Wilson's *The Trials of Margaret Lindsay* (1823) with its ludicrously artificial picture of the fallen, scarlet woman as the depth of human degradation, the symbol of irretrievable social and moral ruin for Walter Lindsay, to see in Hogg's Clifford a symbol of the very opposite. She rescues Basil at the end from degradation. She is the only source of goodness constant in the novel. No wonder that Hogg's story was disliked; but one cannot help but think wryly now that both in content, with its anti-hypocrisy and honesty, and in the freshness of style, in its brevity, its simple language, its swift action, that it was exactly the influence needed to correct the wordy conventionality of the nineteenth-century novel. For Hogg it was a necessary stage towards *The Justified Sinner*. It is also one of his most neglected works.[36]

NOTES

1. *The Spy: A Periodical Paper of Literary Amusement and Instruction* appeared in 52 weekly numbers from Saturday, 1st September 1810. Copies are extremely rare, but that of St. Andrews University Library has articles attributed to their authors in Hogg's handwriting. Hogg's fiction and sketches in *The Spy* magazine 1810/11 comprised:

Nos. III-IV, "On Instability in One's Calling" (revised, as *Basil Lee*) (S). No. VII, "Fictitious Letter to the Spy from Alice Brand" and "Fanny Lively." No. XII introduces the persona of John Miller, the Nithsdale Shepherd who gives the "Description of a Peasant's Funeral" (S) (NF). No. XIII, John Miller's account of a visit to the Theatre (NF); "The Death of Major MacPherson" (reprinted as "The Dreadful Story of MacPherson") (S). No. XVI, Autobiography of the Spy (expanded into "The Love Adventures of Mr George Cochrane") (S). No. XVII, "The Story of Two Highlanders" (S). No. XVIII, John Miller tells "The Story of the Ghost of Lochmaben" (revised as "The Wife of Lochmaben") (S). Nos. XXIV, XXV, XXVI, John Miller tells "The Country Laird" (revised as "The Woolgatherer") (S). No. XXIX, "Impatience under Misfortunes" (revised as "The School of Misfortune" in *The Shepherd's Calendar*). No. XXXV, "The Love of Fame" (revised as "Adam Bell") (S); "Fictitious Letter from A. Solomon." No. XLVII, "Evil Speaking Ridiculed by an Allegorical Dream" (revised as "A Singular Dream") (S). Nos. XLIX, LI, "Duncan Campbell" (S).

All the material marked (S) was collected in *Winter Evening Tales*, 1820. (NF) means non-fiction.

2. *Spy,* no. XIII, 24 November, p. 98.

3. "Malises's Journey to the Trossachs," *Spy,* no. XL, 1 June, p. 313 ff; continued in *Spy,* XLIV, 29 June. There are some most amusing and ironic glimpses of the "stage-managing" of the tourist attraction of the landscape that Scott had popularised, like the "brownie" hired to caper for the benefit of steamer passengers on Loch Ketturin (Katrine).

4. From Hogg's *Autobiography,* which expanded in stages from a memoir first published in *The Mountain Bard.* I have used the final version, which is printed in volume II of Thomson's edition of his works, pp. 441-468, and the quotation is on p. 447.

5. *Spy,* LII, p. 412.

6. *Tales,* vol. II, p. 83.   8. *Tales,* vol. I, p. 17.

7. *Tales,* vol. II, p. 4.   9. *Tales,* vol. I, p. 14.

10. At least one later Scottish novelist was profoundly impressed by Hogg's convincing account of the atrocities. In one of his best novels, *The Men of the Moss Haggs* (1895), which deals with the same theme, S. R. Crockett virtually "lifts" the entire scene for his chapter nine, pp. 66-74.

11. *Tales*, vol. I, p. 42.

12. *Tales*, vol. I, pp. 46-47. See also the poem *Mess John* in *The Mountain Bard, Works*, vol. II, pp. 74-79.

13. *Tales*, vol. I, pp. 63-70.

14. *Tales*, vol. I, p. 73.   15. *Tales*, vol. 1, p. 73.

16. In a letter to Laidlaw of 1818, quoted in *Strout*, p. 150.

17. *Tales*, vol. II, p. 3.   19. *Tales*, vol. II, p. 23.

18. *Tales*, vol. II, p. 6.   20. *Tales*, vol. II, p. 16.

21. *Domestic Manners*, p. 77.

22. George Kitchin, "The Fiction of John Galt," in *Edinburgh Essays on Scots Literature*, 1933, p. 115. "A cruel fidelity to the facts of distraught or diseased temper is undoubtedly a characteristic of these efforts. How general the distemper was may be judged from the fact that Scott's son-in law, Lockhart, wrote two of these repulsive studies . . . Hogg's *Suicide's Grave* [*The Justified Sinner*] is of the same pathological kind. . . ."

23. *Spy*, I, p. 3.

24. *The Justified Sinner*, 1947, ed., pp. 13-14.

25. *Spy*, XXIX, pp. 226-231. It has not hitherto been noticed that this and "Evil Speaking ridiculed by an Allegorical Dream," *Spy*, XLVIII, were revised and reprinted as "The School of Misfortune" in *The Shepherd's Calendar*, 1829 (*Tales*, vol. II, pp. 109-114) and "A Singular Dream" in *Winter Evening Tales*, 1820.

26. *Tales*, vol. II, pp. 109-110.

27. *Tales*, vol. II, pp. 137-198.   29. *Tales*, vol. II, p. 27.

28. *Batho*, p. 119.   30. *Tales*, vol. II, p. 28.

31. *Winter Evening Tales*, vol. I, p. 10. Hogg amended this tale, so that the 1837 *Tales and Sketches*, and consequently the 1886 *Tales*, do not have this scene. It is yet another example of the effect of criticism of Hogg's work as being vulgar and in bad taste.

32. *Tales*, vol. II, p. 35.   34. *Tales*, vol. II, p. 45.

33. *Tales*, vol. II, p. 37.   35. *Tales*, vol. II, p. 35.

36. I have just learned that a new edition of *The Brownie of Bodsbeck* will appear in 1976. Its editor, Douglas Mack, has been so kind as to send me his introduction, in which he concludes that Hogg's novel *was*, after all, probably finished in 1813 and thus before Scott's *Old Mortality*. His discussion of the novel is most valuable.

CHAPTER FOUR

THE THREE PERILS OF MAN (1822) AND
THE THREE PERILS OF WOMEN (1823)

BETWEEN THE *Winter Evening Tales* of 1820 and the
appearance of *The Three Perils of Man* in 1822 Hogg
must have felt confident in his own powers. The *Tales*
had been well received, albeit that praise was directed
towards the shorter stories and sketches, the material
that a talented, "heaven-taught" shepherd could be
expected to collect, as the sub-title described, "among
the Cottagers in the South of Scotland," and not
towards the two short novels therein. His *Jacobite
Relics* (1819), collected in the Highlands, had extended
to a second series with Blackwood which was due out
in 1821, and Constable was bringing out his *Poetical
Works* in four volumes in 1822. Since 1815 he had
been living rent-free as the result of a gift for life by
the Duke of Buccleuch of Altrive Lake Farm. From
this safe, modest base in his beloved Borders he must
have felt that his two careers, of shepherd farmer
and writer, were enhancing each other. At forty-nine,
still in his physical prime, he married; and the following
year was optimistic enough to take out a nine-year
lease on Mount Benger farm, adjacent to Altrive
Lake. It was in this exhilarating period he started
The Three Perils of Man. As he worked on it he was
sure that it was in his best style, possibly better.
Ironically, far from being the accepted masterpiece
of his fiction when it appeared, it was to be the turning
point in that process of disillusionment and critical
neglect which was to lead him to abandon ambitions of
being a major novelist within two years. Ironically,

too, his farming ambitions were to suffer similar set-backs with Mount Benger, which had been the ruin of two farmers there before him. In the course of his lease he was to lose over two thousand pounds on it.

The Three Perils of Man is Hogg's most ambitious work of fiction. Its range, its variety of characters, its wealth of fast action, are all on a scale far beyond even *The Justified Sinner* or *The Brownie of Bodsbeck.* But more significant still, it marks Hogg's courageous and epic attempt to work in the oral and popular tradition which had produced the Ballads, folk-tales and legends. It also marks the passing of this tradition as a living force. Ironically, the society which marvelled at 'Scottland," which had enthused over MacPherson's *Ossian,* had little time for the popular tradition which Hogg represented.

In the context of Hogg's own development, *The Three Perils of Man* represents the burgeoning of his deep interest in that other class of the supernatural, the world of "diablerie" and demonology, the world of Barnaby's tales in "The Woolgatherer," or *The Hunt of Eildon,* the world which he had treated with rationalistic reservations in *The Brownie of Bodsbeck.* It is the world of Will o' Phaup, his grandfather, who had spoken on sundry occasions with the fairies; not just of "spectres, ghosts, fairies, brownies . . . seen and heard . . . in the Glen o' Phaup," but a larger imaginative world which included long tales of "kings, knights, fairies, kelpies . . .", where history is transmuted to legend and recorded in the ballad idiom of timeless, racy, understated simplicity. It is important to understand how solid a foundation this is to the romance. To dismiss the work as mere cloak-and-dagger nonsense is to betray ignorance of the difference between the traditional and folk treatment of things supernatural and the neo-Gothic treatment of, say, *Melmoth the Wanderer* (1820), an ignorance that critics in Hogg's time and since have frequently betrayed in assessing his fiction.

The opening of the novel is in Scott's manner:

> The days of the Stuarts . . . were the days of chivalry and romance. The long and bloody contest that the nation maintained against the whole power of England, for the recovery of its independence—of those rights which had been most unwarrantably wrested from our fathers by the greatest and most treacherous sovereign of that age, . . . laid the foundation [of this chivalry]. The deeds of the Douglases, the Randolphs and other border barons of that day, are not to be equalled. . . .[1]

Scott-like, but there is a difference. Hogg is altogether more racy and terse. He is the biased Borderer, seeing the King of England as "most treacherous," telling epic stories of the Randolphs and Douglases, as Barbour, Blind Harry, and the Border Ballads told them. He describes how anti-English and chivalrous games spread from barons to schoolboys, even to the very ploughmen and peasants. And thus the whole of his story of the chivalric Game of the siege of Roxburgh is based on "national mania," beginning an ironic comment which runs as a major counter-theme, mocking the superficial romance of chivalry.

This pattern of romance offset by realism begins immediately. First we are given the romantic and fairy-tale opening:

> There was once a noble king and queen of Scotland, as many in that land have been . . . beloved by all their subjects . . . and loved and favoured them in

> return; and the country enjoyed happiness and
> peace. . . .[2]

This is surely how Hogg's mother began. And the
signs of a traditional mode of storytelling are abundant.
There is, for example, the ballad emphasis on number;
the castle of Roxburgh

> had been five times taken by the English, and three
> times by the Scots, in less than seventeen months,
> and was then held by the gallant Lord Musgrave
> for Richard King of England.[3]

The King of Scotland's daughter, "of exquisite beauty
and accomplishments," is "the flower of all Scotland."
The Game of Chivalry is set in motion by the folk-tale
condition Margaret lays down for the winning of her
hand. The King, as in "Sir Patrick Spens," "sat gloomy
and sad," and asks which of his nobles will revenge
him on Musgrave. Predictably, the price of failure is
the forfeiture of "lands, castles, towns and towers."
And the richness of detail of the folk-tale is there too
—Margaret's left arm swings a scarf of gold, her right
"gleamed with bracelets of rubies and diamonds."

This is the world of romance and nobility. But like
so many folk-tales and Ballads, the action now moves
to direct, vigorous characters. We meet Sir Ringan
Redhough and his Border reivers, with their ironic
realism. On being asked to help in the Game,
Ringan's attitude is in explicit ironic contrast to the
previous chivalry.

> What, man, are a' my brave lads to lie in bloody
> claes that the Douglas may lie i' snow white sheets
> wi' a bonny bed-fellow? . . . Tell him to keep their
> hands fu'; and their haunches toom, an' they'll soon
> be blithe to leave the lass an' loup at the ladle. . . .[4]

The "flower" of Scotland is reduced to a "bonny bedfellow"; romantic love is seen as a curable disease. Ringan's recommendations are to use "wiles" instead of chivalric methods. And in the savage irony of the juxtaposition of "bloody claes" (death) and "snow white sheets" (sexual pleasure), the one being the price of the other, we meet again the idiom of *Sir Patrick Spens,* with its ironic juxtaposition of the "fingers white" and "goud kaims" against the floating hats and feather beds at the ballad's end.

Similarly, when we meet the main "hero" of the romance, Charlie Scott of Yardbire, the amiable giant, he is breaking up the courtly pattern of the Game. With colossal strength he hurls a knight *and* his horse backwards; and his "tak ye that, master, for whistling o' Sundays" exactly sums up the reductive idiom of much of Hogg's anti-romantic theme. It is all in the peasant tradition of wry humour and worldliness seen in the ballads, chapbooks and "fabliau" tales of lower class medieval Europe, with something of the pace and ferocity of Smollett's action, and it would certainly sound vulgar to polite Edinburgh.

There is one major weakness to be found in Hogg's contrast of these two worlds. It is that he is frequently unsure of his artistic intention and of his own sympathies as he deals with Douglas and Musgrave on one hand, Redhough and Charlie on the other. While it is valid to identify an ironic attitude to chivalry in Hogg's comments through Redhough, the Chisholm family or Charlie, it would be wrong to conclude that Hogg intended us to mock at the world of kings and knights *in toto.* All too often it seems that real sympathy for Douglas or Margaret is intended, and that certain aspects of their chivalrous undertaking are at least countenanced by Hogg. The irony is less controlled, more local and episodic, than that say, of Scott's *Waverley*.

This unsureness may reflect Hogg's own divided loyalties and insecurity about his social position; whatever its source, it blurs the dividing line between straightforward presentation of romance and ironic comment upon it. But we should not make too much of this weakness, because it would be a parsimonious reading of Hogg's romance that failed to realise that its unity lies not in aspects of plot structure, or carefully planned revelation of character through action, but in something looser, larger and much more uncommon in the nineteenth century. C. S. Lewis made a special plea that another Scottish writer of profound and vivid imagination, George MacDonald, should be assessed on the special considerations that his work went far beyond typical areas of fiction to myth. Hogg is just such a special case. And the strange unity that his work possesses comes, not from qualities of myth (although it occasionally attains this) but from its sheer extravagant and fantastic gusto and the obvious enjoyment of the author in allowing his imagination free rein. Thus we do not object to the ridiculous disguises of Princess Margaret and Lady Jane Howard when they arrive at the Chisholm's house; and thus Hogg gets away with the more serious ambiguity underlying the latter scene when Margaret, discovering who "Sir Jasper" is, sends her prisoner by Charlie Scott to Douglas.

This is a typically difficult and ambiguous passage. On one hand it would seem that Hogg is ironically reducing his knights and ladies to the level of barbarians and fishwives—as when the two girls coarsely and spitefully attack each other. They become merely spoiled girls. Similarly Douglas, knowing full well the identity of his captive, ignores her pleas to his "honour and generosity as a knight" and forces her to strip—or later promises to cause her to be "exhibited in a state not to be named" on a stage erected in sight of the western tower, raped publicly ("disgrace which barbarians only could have conceived"), "and then to have her nose cut off, her eyes put out, and her beauteous frame otherwise disfigured."

How are we to read this? It is tempting to attribute to Hogg a greater degree of deliberate anti-romantic irony than exists. It would seem as though Hogg's attitude is never resolved, because on the other hand there is plenty of description of Douglas and the ladies as genuinely noble and romantic creatures—witness how the end of the novel has Charlie and Sir Ringan rewarded by these very princes and ladies. And this is why the final case for the greatness of the work lies *beyond* consideration of the sophistication or otherwise of the ironic structure, in the sheer zest of the persentation and the speed of the metamorphoses and reversals of fortune. The principal consideration of the tale's worth lies in its qualities as a tale to be told as Hogg's mother told him tales.

But the irony is nevertheless deliberate and fine at many points. There can be no doubt of Hogg's meaning and where his sympathies lie in the hanging of the servants of Lady Jane. The Game of Roxburgh is death to the English peasant Heaton and his friends; the spoiled heiresses of Scotland and England have more or less murdered many like him by the time the Game is over. Immediately following this, as though to prove the point, is the episode of the old Border fisherman, Sandy Yellowlees, one of Hogg's well-loved, independent heroes. Hogg tricks us into identifying with Sandy. His peasant humour, his comic fears when he starts finding sirloins of beef on the end of his line, and the fact that he is permitted to use the dramatic monologue to tell his story—a method Hogg generally reserves for favourites—contribute towards a shock of revulsion against the chivalrous siege, when, with the swordstroke suddenness of the ballads, Sandy is captured and hanged from the walls of Roxburgh castle.

And part one ends on this sarcastic note. Savagery and madness dominate the starving castle. A group of mutineers are "hanged like dogs, amid shouts of execration, and their bodies flung into a pit," while the remainder adopt cannibalism rather than surrender. Chivalry has become nightmare. Hogg now draws the English under Musgrave in a stylised, grotesque fashion, suggesting bestial gargoyles, far from concepts of courtly love.

> There they sat, a silent circle, in bitter and obstinate rumination. Their brows were plaited down, so as to almost cover their eyes; their underlips were bent upwards and every mouth shaped like a curve, and their arms were crossed on their breasts, while every man's right hand instinctively rested on the hilt of his sword . . . a wild gleam of ferocity fired every haggard countenance.[5]

Whether instinctive or deliberate, Hogg's ironic picture of how the Game had lost any semblance of a chivalrous contest is effective.

The second part, that concerning the comic embassy's journey to the wizard, Sir Michael Scott, releases Hogg from the juxtaposition of romantic and realistic attitudes. Indeed the term "release" well describes the extended nightmare, comic and fantastic, which follows, with the pace and spirit of Dunbar's demonological poems and Burns's "Tam o' Shanter."

Sir Ringan, needing to know something of the outcome of the struggle before he decides which side to favour, sends his representatives to find out. His embassy is grotesque, a freakish collection of oddities and misfits to please the unnatural tastes of Michael Scott. He sends—

> as a bard, or minstrel, . . . Colley Carol, a man that is fit to charm the spirits out of the heart of the earth, or the bowels of the cloud . . . as a man of crabbed wit and endless absurdity . . . the Deil's Tam; as a truly natural and moral philosopher, the laird o' the Peatstacknowe; as one versed in all the mysteries of religion, and many mysteries besides, or some tell lies, we can send the gospel friar. All these are men of spirit, and can handle the sword and the bow. . . . And as a man of unequalled strength and courage, and a guard and captain over all the rest, we can send Charlie o' Yardbire. And I will defy all the kingdoms of Europe to send out sic another quorum either to emperor, Turk, wizard or the devil himself.[6]

Add the captive maiden Delany, and the beautiful boy Elias, and the embassy is complete. And it is this parody of the character of the usual reiving party that makes the comedy so rich. The story now becomes mock-epic; a motley crew on a fantastic quest, a travesty of the Canterbury pilgrims. Not only is the medieval idea of the journey used to comic effect, but sometimes even the various characters, like the Deil's Tap especially, seem to be almost medieval personifications of human qualities. Tam, standing for Greed and Famine in one, takes part in a Dunbar-like dance of Sin, although, unlike Dunbar, Hogg mixes good and bad in his increasingly wild movement. Adventure follows adventure with the speed of Smollett; violence flares suddenly and dies as quickly. There is little complexity of situation now—apart from the pretty obvious hints that the dour and mysterious friar is more than he seems. And yet—probably because the embassy is mainly made up of Borderers and dominated by the refreshingly unusual hero, Charlie Scott—there is complete clarity of character delineation within the group, even down to the mule, wilful and almost human (considered by Lockhart to be the real hero of the romance).

We begin to have a curious feeling of completeness about the group of contrasting characters. A pattern emerges, with Charlie as Honesty and Strength, the Friar as Faith, Gibby as Clown and Weakness generally (for which he is claimed as temporary servant by Scott), and Tam as Greed and Fleshly Lust (he signs his soul away to the devil). The framework is at once definite and yet loose enough to permit the contrasting idioms —the Friar's Chaldee style, contrived and Ossianic, the poet's flowery excesses, Charlie's blunt but compassionate realism, and Tam's bald, horrifyingly honest directness.

We have moved from the world of chivalry, with its rules and conditions, to a world of topsy-turvey, with its own weird rules, patently dominated by a Lord of Misrule. And Hogg achieves the transition by capturing the unnatural atmosphere around Scott's castle of Aikwood at sunset:

It was one of those dead calm winter evenings, not uncommon at that season, when the slightest noise is heard at a distance, and the echoes are all abroad.

110

As they drew near to the huge darklooking pile, silence prevailed among them more and more. All was so still that even the beautiful valley seemed a waste. There was no bird whistling at the plough; no cattle or sheep grazing on the holms of Aikwood; no bustle of servants, kinsmen, or their grooms, as at the castles of other knights. It seemed as if the breath of the enchanter, or his eye, had been infectious, and had withered all within its influence, whether of vegetable, animal, or human life. The castle itself scarcely seemed to be the abode of man; the massy gates were all locked . . . and there was only one small piping smoke issuing from one of the turrets.[7]

From now on metamorphoses occur on every second page. Gourlay is transformed by Scott by way of punishment into a hare, and frenziedly pursued by the attendant devils, Prim, Prig and Pricker, who transform themselves with bewildering speed. An army of retainers marches from the wainscoting of the deserted castle to serve breakfast to the embassy, who are struck by their "rattan faces." And in one of the funniest of these transformations, the company are led from the raw and misty morning up into a tower room which blazes with light; the tables groan with smoking sirloins of beef "with a gentle brown crust around it, and half swimming in gravy. . . ." Most of the embassy start without saying grace: the friar, later to enter,

lifted up his spread hands, closed his eyes, and leaning forward above the beef so closely that he actually breathed upon it, felt the flavour of health and joy ascending by his nostrils [and] in that

111

fervent and respectful attitude he blessed the beef in the name of Jesus.

Never had blessing a more dolorous effect. When the friar opened his eyes, the beef was gone. There was nothing left on the great wooden plate before him but a small insignificant thing resembling the joint of a frog's legs, or that of a rat; and perhaps two or three drops of gravy. . . .[8]

Metamorphosis dominates this part, from the curious use of the magic lantern which anticipates the nightmare scene on Salisbury crags in *The Justified Sinner,* to the final banquet with the devil and Michael Scott, where hags with withered chops are transformed into beauteous ladies, and the men of the embassy into bellowing bulls.

Slowly, from the apparently formless, though vastly entertaining, riot of diablerie and nightmare, the theme of this part emerges. We are witnessing an epic, yet still comic, struggle between the powers of Light and Dark. First of all the "seconds" meet. The monstrous Gourlay, seneschal-zombie of Scott, possessed of superhuman strength, clashes with the benevolent giant Charlie Scott. Their epic battle takes place in a vault where the giant bones of a previous victim lie gleaming in the moonlight. With an impact like that of Beowulf and Grendel in its almost mythical stature, they meet in titanic battle. Gourlay's back and ribs sound as they crack; his face grows hideous; they fall ponderously amidst the bones of the giant skeleton. The entire situation reminds one of Bunyan's *Pilgrim's Progress,* with Gourlay as Giant Despair.

Following this preparatory round, we anticipate the confrontation of the friar, man of mysterious depths, and the wizard. Both have epic features, especially

Michael Scott, with his dignity, his respect for courage, his occasional sympathy, as when he hears the friar's tragic tale, contrasting with his unholy glee or despair, or his inability, like Faust, to repent. There is greatness in Hogg's imagination here; Michael is conceived on a superhuman scale, as is the account at the end of the romance of his cataclysmic exit from this world. His battle with the friar lives up to our expectations. Indeed, it may not be stretching the scene too much to find a deeper layer within it The friar uses science; the magic lantern, tricks with chemicals, and finally his superbly fitting and comic removal of the monster Gourlay by blowing him up with gunpowder (which, as the exiled Roger Bacon, he's supposed to have invented). Scott uses sheer wizardry and the power of the devil. Do we see here the division in Hogg's own allegiance to nineteenth-century rationalism and scientific achievement on the one hand, and to a belief in the supernatural forces of the past on the other, as in the subtler psychological and supernatural ambiguity of *The Justified Sinner*? In any event, although the friar triumphs initially, there is no doubt that Hogg's deepest sympathies are with Michael, goaded by the friar beyond endurance, to the point where he almost overstretches his remit from the devil. Hogg's imagination blends here in superb fashion with his awareness of Border legend. He postulates a single, unbroken Eildon hill, a great cone, prior to the battle. The wizard orders Prim, Prig and Pricker to twist it into three (as the mountain is now). The ensuing storm is a colossal reversal of nature (it is the storm in which the Scots were attacked by the maddened English at the end of part one).

What makes this sensational "diablerie" so acceptable is the comic, but realistic and matter-of-fact way

Hogg tells it all. It is exactly right for the extravagant, richly coloured imaginary world he has made, and sustains the supernatural so well that the effect has nothing of the neo-gothic wildness of *The Castle of Otranto* (1764). Hogg is saved from this by the fact that his own rich imagination is based firmly on folk tradition, which he uses in a vital and creative way. The Eildon hill scene is the best of these. Hogg's picture of the pallid, unnatural dawn following the turmoil of the night, with the friar and Charlie frozen in astonishment at the three peaks towering over new rivers is a magnificent climax, almost mythic in quality. His imagination sees it surely and follows through without faltering:

> It was a scene of wonder not to be understood, and awfully impressive. The two rivers flowed down their respective valleys, and met below the castle like two branching seas, and every little streamlet roared and foamed like a river. The hills had a wan, bleached appearance, many of the trees of the forest were shivered, and towering up against the eastern sky, there stood the three . . . hills of Eildon, where before there was but one.[9]

The next part, which begins with the discovery that the embassy and Scott are trapped in the castle tower, does bulk too large in the overall story. It may be that Hogg, remembering his great success with the situation of a competition of raconteurs in *The Queen's Wake*, his long poem of 1813, tried to repeat it here. He certainly loved the exercise of adopting different styles and *personas* in storytelling (witness *The Spy* and the three points of view in *The Justified Sinner*) and poetry (witness his *Poetic Mirror* of 1816). Or it may simply be the case that he had some of these short stories

114

already written, and decided to incorporate them, using the simple expedient of Scott's proposal, that they should relieve their plight by storytelling, the best storyteller winning Delany, the worst being eaten by the others.

It can be argued that these tales, like *The Canterbury Tales,* play a part in telling us something about the tellers. The friar's tale solves the mystery of the strange affinity between the worn old friar and the innocent Delany—she is the daughter of his sweetheart. And the Ossianic style has the function of contrasting refreshingly with the romance's usual, more direct idiom. Hogg's romance is loose enough in structure and fantastic enough in content to stand casual storytelling, and highly coincidental revelations like this. Indeed, the story has a certain tragic pathos and power. It reveals yet again Charlie's sentimental nature. It causes the poet to change his mind about hating the friar. And when Delany reveals she is the friar's sweetheart's daughter, "even Master Michael Scott once drew the back of his hand across his eyes. . . ."

In stark contrast is the savage tale told by the Laird of Peatstacknowe; harsh, unsentimental, chapbookish in its crude caricature of Marion's son Jock who "fought to be at meat, and Marion to keep him from it; and many hard clouts and claws there passed." Jock is a recurrent type in Hogg's stories. There is something unnatural in his demonic hunger, his utter amorality—compare him with Basil Lee, or Merodach the Brownie of the Black Haggs, or the Justified Sinner himself. And Hogg is unsurpassed when it comes to describing sordid violence with sickeningly convincing detail. Jock's master wants to kick and beat him, and then murder him; he drags him to the lamb Jack has murdered, where again the remains, like those of an outraged daughter, madden him; he throws him down, kneels on him, punches till Jock

> got hold of his master's cheek with his left hand, and his nails being very long . . . was like to tear it off. His master capered up with his head . . .[10]

and, unable to free himself, gets out his knife to cut off Jock's hand—and then his head. The savagery is conveyed in the factual imagery, the bald statement of fact; the battle is "like a battle between an inveterate terrier and a bull dog," and is ended suddenly and shockingly when Jock—merely a boy—

> whipped out his own knife, his old dangerous friend, and stuck it into the goodman's belly to the haft. The moment he received the wound he sprang up as if he had been going to fly into the air, uttered a loud roar, and fell back above his dead pet lamb.[11]

The scene reminds one of the violent end of the sensual fox in Robert Henryson's *The Fox, the Wolf and the Cadger.* The slightly comic tone accentuates the violence [Jock uses his "dangerous friend" to kill the goodman] as does the understatement. And, like Henryson's *Fables,* the violence is more shocking, coming as it does in a pastoral setting: Jock's anxious mother, the scene in the goodman's cottage of family eating, the shepherding—all assert the countryside quality of rhythms repeating themselves peacefully. The violence is in horrible contrast to all this, as are the sensual descriptions of Jock's hunger and the goodman's misplaced, unnatural grief, over his pet lamb.

And all this is *embodied* in the main development of the surrounding story. Hogg reveals that Jock, this monster of carnal hunger, this unnatural child-demon, is the Deil's Tam. With one easy move, Tam's evil takes on a new depth, and his fate grows darker. And again the reactions of the others reveal their characters. Charlie thinks it a good tale—"o' the kind" he stresses; the poet, sensitive plant as he is, accepts the lamb-daughter equation, and is horrified at the eating of "the flower of all the flock . . . her lovely form that's fairer than the snow." And in fact many of the others accept this symbolism too; as Michael Scott says:

> The maid Delany is the favourite lamb, whom he wishes you to kill and feast on . . . and I am the Goodman whom you are to stick afterwards. . . .[12]

Charlie Scott's tale is a good example of Hogg's mastery of the story of action, related by one of his favourite border heroes of the Wat o' Chapelhope cast. It is another Ballad story, close to "The Battle of Otterbourne" in its qualities of stern bravery and feudal devotion. It also reveals Charlie's goodness in his saving of a child in a raid—who turns out to be the poet. Thus this story, like the others, relates to the main theme in that it extends our knowledge of the characters in the embassy and supplies answers to Hogg's beloved mysteries. Charlie's tale is good; its qualities are those found abundantly throughout Hogg's tales, notably in the later "Mary Montgomery" and "Wat Pringle o' the Yair."

Tam's tale reveals that he is the "Marion's Jock" of Gibby's story. Tam is completed by this as a character personifying greed and lust. His story, with its savagery and cruelty and anti-heroic qualities, provides a contrast to Charlie's tale of healthy heroism, in the same way that Basil Lee or Robert Wringhim are the utter opposite of Wat o' Chapelhope of *The Brownie of Bodsbeck*. These types are recurrent polarities in

Hogg's fiction, and Tam's story is one of his many horrifying pictures of amoral, lustful and utterly wicked men. Ironically, Tam does in fact become "the Deil's Tam."

Nevertheless, although many of the tales are good in themselves (the poet's being the weakest), and although they do contribute towards the development of relationships amongst the group, they do distract us from the main, hitherto swift-moving plot. It is a relief for the reader, as well as for the trapped embassy, when Dan Chisholm and his Border friends arrive at the castle. Hogg now links his two projects, and we see Scott's wizardry through fresh eyes.

> Do nae ye ken that the world's amaist turned upside down sin ye left us? The trees hae turned their wrang ends upmost—the waters hae drowned the towns, and the hills hae been rent asunder. . . . Tis thought that there has been a siege o' hell. . . .[13]

says Dan—there are devils loose. The reign of Disorder is not yet over; Dan and Charlie now meet a mysterious friend of Sir Michael Scott's. Unlike the friend Gilmartin, who is sinister from his very bland sophistication, this superb devil is in the manner of the demonology of the Ballads.

> It appeared about double the human size . . . its whole body being of the colour of bronze, as well as the crown upon its head. The skin appeared shrivelled, as if seared with fire, but over that there was a polish that glittered and shone. Its eyes had no pupil nor circle of white; they appeared like burning lamps deep in their sockets; and when it gazed, they rolled round. . . . There was a hairy mantle that hung down and covered its feet . . . every

> finger . . . terminated in a long crooked talon that
> seemed of the colour of molten gold. . . . It had
> neither teeth, tongue, nor throat, its whole inside
> being hollow, and the colour of burning glass. . . [14]

It pursues them, vomiting burning sulphur; and, as the
nightmare climax of Disorder is reached, "immense
snakes, bears, tigers and lions, all with eyes like
burning candles" threaten the heroes. Hogg here draws
from sources as different as Bunyan and the Ballads.
This last supernatural climax, with its strange,
glittering beauty of imagery, so close to the clarity and
concrete visualisation of the Ballads, proves completely
Hogg's right to claim that he was King of the Mountain
and Fairy school of poets, in its description of how
Dan meets the Devil and agents disguised as a Black
Abbot on terrible white horses; how the Devil wanders
in a village as a great shaggy black dog, terrifying
peasants; how Dan and his friends undergo a nightmare ride through the firmament; how the devil plays
on the weakness of Charlie and his friends for drink
and lovely women, seducing their senses with a superficial beauty like that in Dunbar's "The Twa Maryit
Women and the Wedo," a beauty corrupt and foul
beneath its surface; and how this beauty reveals its
essential rottenness when the drunken Borderers realise
that the lovely girls are hags with rotten teeth and
wizened faces. The Devil, as a final, glorious flourish
of Disorder, finishes the long dance by transforming
them all into bulls.

All this is told with a dry attention to details mixed
with a strange and beautiful description of the trappings
of evil. Like the author of "The Daemon Lover," who
is fascinated by the gold and silver, the "taffetie" of
the ship's sails, Hogg clearly sees the rich colours of his

devils—yet combines this with a touchingly homely reminder of Charlie's consideration for his horse, Corby, or the honest joy of Charlie at realising that his Border lord and friends hadn't forgotten him. And it is Charlie who characteristically persists through all terrors to secure the prophecy for Sir Ringan which is the point of his embassy, while Gibby is claimed by Sir Michael to replace Gourlay, and Tam literally becomes "the Deil's" in a temptation scene which foreshadows the sinner's selling of his soul, the nightmare climax of *The Justified Sinner*.

The final part cannot match the richness of this fantasy and diablerie, though the return to the Siege of Roxburgh contains at least two episodes, those of the affair of Dan Chisholm and the cattle skins and the actual taking of the castle by borderers disguised as cattle, which for sheer speed of action of racy dialogue and character are as good as any short story of Hogg's. And this last episode marks the final irony of the Siege, for Douglas at last confesses that the chivalrous Game has beaten him. He has to descend to "wiles," and to ask Sir Ringan to do it for him while he takes no part. The chivalrous pattern has finally been wrecked, as Lady Howard is destined to become the wife of Charlie, the homely Borderer. Musgrave has killed himself, Douglas has hardly succeeded on his own merits, and Princess Margaret is presumed hanged.

But it is worth noting that the last part does hold together with the demonology. For Sir Ringan finally acts because of the success of Charlie's embassy and Sir Michael Scott's (and the Devil's) advice; and his ruse of disguising his men comes from the metamorphosis of Charlie and his men into bulls. Hogg has been aware of the strain of his range of plots and characters—indeed, he stresses that the final ironic burst of Border warfare which finishes the siege

> was wholly owing to the weird read by the great enchanter master Michael Scott. So that though the reader must have felt that Isaac [the curate narrator] kept his guests too long in that horrible place the Castle of Aikwood, it will now appear that not one iota of that long interlude of his could have been omitted; for till the weird was read, and the transformation consummated the embassy could not depart—and unless these had been effected, the castle could not have been taken. . . .[15]

Elsewhere Hogg had likened his problem in controlling his multitude of characters and situations to that of the waggoner who has to take his total load up a steep hill in stages, going back to collect what had to be left behind. These arguments do less to justify his structure than to tell us about his awareness of the difficulties in controlling the whole immense undertaking. He tells us in his *Domestic Manners of Sir Walter Scott* that he and Scott discussed the romance, Scott accusing him of rushing impatiently on in random fashion, and thus spoiling a potentially good tale. Whether we agree with Scott or not, Hogg's statement here about his method of composition is highly significant. He told Scott that when he started the first line of a tale or a novel, he never knew what the second was to be, and that this continued throughout. But he made an important qualification.

> When my tale is traditionary, the work is easy, as I then see my way before me, though the tradition be ever so short, but in all my prose works of the imagination, knowing little of the world, I sail on without star or compass.[16]

With qualification, this can fairly be applied to *The Three Perils of Man*. The sense of tradition does contribute to some of the finest passages of the work—especially those relating to Sir Michael Scott. It is the connections between episodes and interpolated short stories that show Hogg on less sure ground.

But there are two aspects of Hogg's statement with which one cannot agree. Firstly, he overmodestly credits "tradition" with the success of his work, and seems to belittle his own imagination, whereby he is grossly unfair to himself and his romance. For when one has pointed out Hogg's awareness of the Ballad and folk-tale tradition, when one has drawn parallels with *The Pilgrim's Progress* or the chapbooks, one vital factor remains to astonish the critic. It is simply the sheer fecundity, immensity and colour of Hogg's imagination, which, working on all kinds of traditional material, creates a living world which needs no other justification than its own unique blend of irony, racy humour, fantasy and romance.

And secondly, it can be argued that the book, far from lacking overall shape, a "sailing on without star or compass," is instead very unified, in a demonstrable fashion, by parallels, contrasts and constant themes. The middle fantasy part is closely allied to its two surrounding parts. It is worth noting these briefly, to dispel the idea that Hogg had no total control.

For parallels there are the two disguises of the "ladies" and the two disguises of the Chisholm girls; the substitute hanging of the false Musgrove and the substitute hanging of the false Margaret. Castle Roxburgh is paralleled by Castle Aikwood, and sieges of a kind occur at both, while at both there is a constant stress on eating meat and indeed the idea of eating fellow-humans. The factual men-oxen have their counterpart in the magical men-oxen, The Friar is paralleled with Michael, Gourlay with Charlie, Jane with Margaret—the list of parallels which interlock the parts of the book is abundant.

In contrasts, emphasising their technical, unifying rôle rather than their ironic significance, there is the overall setting of heroic against anti-heroic; the real against the false, as in Margaret's being on one hand a conventional Shakespearean disguise-heroine, but also a realistically jealous and proud girl. Similarly there is the repeated contrast between boast and performance, from those made by the courtly warriors to those made by the Magician in his pride, which contrast so unhappily with the results. At times it seems too that Hogg wants the sense of contrast to keep us wondering if anybody or anything is constant —even Charlie can move swiftly from hero and noble warrior to being a buffoon easily scared by magic.

I have already stressed the persistent themes of metamorphosis, disguise, and the way there is constant deception and trickery. When one realises that even the interpolated tales echo recurrent themes in the book, with three "good" tales about rescue from doom set against two "bad" tales about greed and killing, as well as stressing the contrast between appearance and disguise, it becomes obvious that Hogg, whether intuitively or consciously, had within his vision a sense of pattern and unity. There may, after all, be no moral point to the book other than ironic comment on the timeless nature of hypocrisy and affectation on the part of superior classes from the middle ages to polite nineteenth-century Edinburgh, but it is still a unified achievement which is the last major effort of the dying, centuries-old tradition which produced the Ballads, which may go some way to explain the immense sense of elegy about the passing of Michael, which has a power akin to the passing of Arthur. An age has passed away.

It is also wonderful and refreshing entertainment; and there is a typical sly joke behind it all which I failed to notice when I edited the novel. All the sense of quest, of great journeys, of mighty powers being sought out at tremendous risk is, to the reader who looks at a map or knows the Borders, suddenly made ludicrous when he realises that the distance from Ringan Redhough's castle of Mountcomyn to Michael Scott's Aikwood, two of the focal points of the novel, is no more than a dozen miles, with Roxburgh Castle, the third point, about the same again from Aikwood! The storm of chivalry and diablerie has indeed been in a teacup!

Thus by 1822 Hogg had tried to develop a kind of historical romance-cum-mystery, to develop a vigorous vein of psychological anti-romance, and to write a comic epic of the supernatural Border traditions. His efforts were not appreciated. Not even bothering to read the work, the "Noctes Ambrosianae" of the period set the tone of casual prejudgment:

> I dare say 'twill be like all his things,—a mixture of the admirable, the execrable, and the tolerable. . . .

This was probably Lockhart, as Wilson said elsewhere that he would "write a page or two rather funny on Hogg's romance"—obviously not in praise, as he went on to say "though averse to being cut up myself, I like to abuse my friends."[17] Hogg was lucky that Wilson did not follow this up.

What is difficult to understand is Walter Scott's dislike. The man who had himself used goblins, astrologers and the Devil in his tales and poems told

Hogg he had ruined "one of the best tales in the world" with his extravagance in demonology. One would have thought that even for the romance's use of legend and folk-lore alone the interest of Scott the antiquarian would have been aroused. But it would appear that Scott's conception of the kind of supernatural material permissible or desirable for a novelist to use underwent considerable change throughout the eighteen-twenties. Hogg remarked on Scott's turning "renegade" with his stories "made up of half-and-half, like Nathaniel Gow's toddy"—that is, with the supernatural content "watered" to such a point that its very existence was ambiguous. In a review of John Galt's *The Omen,* in *Blackwood's Magazine* of 1826, Scott made this change of view explicit when he laid down a clear distinction, wherein he condemns as unworthy of a man of breeding and education any belief in

> the superstition of the olden time, which believed in spectres, fairies, and other supernatural apparitions. These airy squadrons have long been routed, and are banished to the cottage and the nursery.

Poor Hogg! The living connection of his romance with the Ballad tradition, with folk-tale and the world of vividly realised and colourfully diverse creatures of the superstitious imagination, is here by implication condemned. In some ways Scott's attitude must stand as a watershed in Scottish literature, with Hogg on the wrong side.

After the failure of his Border romance, Hogg, with typical refusal to be disheartened, turned to the one major area of fiction he had not yet tried, the novel of manners. Jane Austen's reputation was growing, aided by Scott's generous admiration, and in Edinburgh itself Susan Ferrier's *Marriage* (1818) and

Mary Brunton's *Emmeline* (1819) would be familiar to Hogg. Scott himself would shortly write his only novel of the kind, *St Ronan's Well* (1824), while Hogg's colleague and friend, John Wilson, had just written the first of his three volumes of fiction which were studies of manners and morals at a humbler (and more sentimental and aesthetically debased) level, *Lights and Shadows of Scottish Life* (1822), to be followed in 1823 by *The Trials of Margaret Lindsay*. All these examples and ideas around him caused Hogg, disastrously, to throw his hat into this ring too. Of all kinds of literature to imitate this, for the man who had attacked the bluestockings of Edinburgh for damning his *Spy* magazine, whose background was so utterly alien to the rarefied atmosphere he was now entering, was the kind most likely to produce grotesque, incongruous and bathetic results.

The Three Perils of Women is really three stories. The first is a full-size novel of manners, the second, tenuously linked through a common character, the Northumberland Charlie-Scott type laird, Dick Rickleton, is a surprisingly moving short story, and the third is an ill-told Jacobite short novel in the manner of Hogg's worst excesses in fiction like *The Bridal of Polmood*. Each relates to a "peril" of women; love, leasing (lying) and jealousy respectively, although the link between "peril" and story is often vague and artificial.

The novel is the study of Gatty Bell, a well-to-do farmer's daughter who seeks Edinburgh high life and love. She falls for the romantic highlander, McIon, but owing to his man-of-feeling reticence, she almost loses him to her elfin cousin, "little Cherry Elliott, full of vivacity . . . and blithe as a lamb," an obvious descendant of Kilmeny and the hosts of impossibly innocent country blossoms in Hogg's poetry that are too pure to stand the gales of cruel life. Through the machinations of Gatty's tough, ambitious mother and other formidable, snobbish ladies, Cherry is induced to surrender McIon to Gatty, but she dies of grief as a result, while Gatty's guilt causes her to fall into a three-year-and-a-day coma. ("Have I been in the grave? Or in a madhouse? Or in the land of spirits?") She has, during this coma, produced a healthy bouncing baby, with whom, after having urged her guilt by her three-year penance (which Hogg implies may have been a case of demonic possession of her body while her spirit has been elsewhere) she is happily united.

The subject matter that made second-rate and would-be transcendental verse in *The Pilgrims of the Sun* appears as completely incongruous when set as here in the prosaic background of a Border farming family and polite Edinburgh, although there is a serious theme underneath, which will be developed into the mental torments of *The Justified Sinner*. There is also the ambiguity of the treatment, in that we never know whether demons or mere mental sickness lies at the bottom of her state. And there is, if we separate the coma situation from the rest of the novel, a traditional atmosphere about her "enchantment."

> The cock crew. It was a still dark morning, and the shrill clarion note rang through every apartment, although it came from a distance. Everyone started, as if touched by electricity. . . . "Is that the first or second crowing?" whispered Mrs Johnson. . . .[18]

In the coma, Gatty's soul is at stake like Robert Wringhim's, and just as Gilmartin and White Lady fight for moral supremacy over him, so here:

127

She shook as if agitated by some demon that knew how to exercise or act upon any one of the human powers . . . the creature sat struggling and writing . . . It appeared as if an angel and a demon had been struggling about the possession of her frame . . . as if sometimes the one held the citadel, and sometimes the other.[19]

But this Ballad eerieness sits awkwardly in Edinburgh, while even more awkward is the shallow adolescence and frivolity of Gatty herself. She is no Wringhim, a powerful mind warped and fascinating. She is a tedious trifler, whose response to her lover's invitation to his Highland home is

O gracious me, no, no! What would I do seeing a country where all the people are papists, rebels, and thieves? Where I could not pronounce one word of the language, not a local name. . . ? How could I ask the name of the road over Drumoachder, or Correiyearach, or Meealfourvounnich? God keep me out of that savage country![20]

And if Hogg is mistaken in thinking that he can present an Emma or even a Juliana, he is even more aesthetically wrong in the way that, for the first time in the development of his fiction, he introduces sentimentalised, stock figures who will become part of the kailyard gallery of stereotypes. Hogg had managed to avoid the temptation to cheapen his country figures, but in Gatty's father Daniel Bell, and in the pasteboard Scotsman McIon he succumbs to the lure of "Scotch novels" which had caused even John Galt to create that nauseating, tear-jerking phony peddler of parish-pump pseudo-morality, *Sir Andrew Wylie* (1822), and was producing the worst of Tory propaganda

through the pen of John Wilson. It is a highly significant drop in Hogg's standards that he allows himself
to exploit the potential of the rough-spoken but
honest, hamely Dandie-Dinmont farmer Daniel Bell.
His mawkish advice to his daughter about Edinburgh
dangers ("ye hae to learn to manage your head, your
hands, your feet, and your heart. . . . It's not the bobs
and curls, the ribbons and the rose knots, the gildit
kames . . . that are to stand the test for life . . ."[21]) or
his couthy descriptions of his dance with Lady Eskdale
show a new, uncomfortable attitude to the Borderer
for Hogg.

> The music strak up wi' a great speed, and aff we
> went, round-about and round-about, back and forret,
> setting to this ane, and setting to the tither—deil hae
> me an I kenned a foot whaur I was gaun . . . like a
> sturdied toop, and the sweat drapping aff at the stirls
> o my nose . . . mare through shame than fatigue. . . .[22]

Comparison of this with the earlier "Shepherd's
Wedding" will set the false against the real. From now
on Hogg increasingly exploited both the image of
himself as Ettrick shepherd and his Border material.
There is honest feeling in the treatment of Daniel, as
in the descriptions of him treating his Sundays as
occasions for thinking of "breeds of tups, prices of
wedders, wool, and crock ewes, till the service was
over . . . thoroughly convinced in his own mind that
religion was an exceedingly good thing."[23] But against
this good-humoured satiric comment on *real* Scottish
attitudes there is all the more anger on the reader's
part for Daniel's reduction to an emaciated tearful old
man, portrayed in the Henry Mackenzie manner, as he
asks his daughter to picture his empty chair. . . .

> Ye'll say, mother, where's my father the night, that
> his plates no set, and his glass a-wanting, and his
> snuff-mill toom . . .[24]

and the Davie Tait prayer idiom is misused for
pathetic, rather than comic, ends, with an eavesdropper
moved to tears. Daniel tells the Lord that he's

> no gaun to prig an' arglebargan wi' ye as ye war a
> Yorkshireman. . . . Ye hae gi'en me wealth, an'
> just as muckle with as to guide it, an' nae mair. Ye
> hae gi'en a wife that's just sic and sae. . . . But ye
> gae me a daughter that has aye been the darling of
> my heart, an' now thou's threatening to take this
> precious gift frae me again, in the very Mayflower
> o' life.[25]

What has happened is that Daniel's original rôle in
the novel, whereby he was the ironic counterweight to
Edinburgh affectation and snobbery, has lapsed. Instead
of continuing the ironic pattern of *The Three Perils
of Man,* with its juxtaposition of peasant and courtly
transposed into modern Edinburgh terms, Hogg has
lost confidence in the theme, and genuine ironic possibility has given way to sentimentalism and a retreat to
safe rôle-playing. The novel, having lost its central
integrity, falls into wild incongruities. It swings with
no warning from pathetic comedy to melodramatic
tragedy, with stuck-on moral exhortations which come
from Mrs Hamilton's *Cottagers of Glenburnie* (1805)
and the host of didactic Mrs Masons, Mrs Mortimers,
Mrs Douglases—and eventually Mrs Grundies—that
that novel spawned in Scotland. Hogg's Mrs Bell warns
her daughter that

> A maid, you know, is a sheet of white paper, and she
> cannot be too careful whom she first suffers to

indorse his name on the pure scroll, for then the erasure is hard to be effected."[26]

The very language with its stiff aridity tells us that Hogg is out of his depth. It is interesting that Hogg handles this lady in a dual fashion. She is at times a successful satiric picture of a hypocritical, domineering targe, snobbish and positively wicked in her dealings with Cherry as she causes the death of her own niece to advance her snobbish designs. Here is the bite and dislike of affectation of *Basil Lee*—but, illustrating perfectly Hogg's failure of confidence at this time, like the picture of Daniel this picture too is altered and allowed to lose its vigour and sting. Mrs Bell is a party to the artificial, happy domestic resolution as a proud and fitting grandmother. The novel's attacks on Edinburgh "puppies," ministers and bluestockings, affectations of dancing masters and dressmakers gives way to a bland and pointless denouement.

The other two tales need not detain us long. The short tale on the peril of "leasing" tells the sequel to the comic wooing of the gigantic clown Richard Rickleton, who sought Gatty's hand in the novel. He marries a woman who turns out to be pregnant by a sleekit, sly Edinburgh lawyer. Hogg may have felt a certain shame in his watering-down of his anti-Edinburgh feeling in the novel, for he certainly reverts here with a vengeance to his *Basil Lee* cocking-of-a-snook against polite Edinburgh, with the same note of real compassion in the way that bluff Dick Rickleton eventually talks himself round to what the reader has known he'll do all along. He accepts the other man's child as his own, forgives the wife, and all without any trace of conditions or moral superiority. Here, refreshingly, is the real Hogg, with a direct

131

frankness of expression and an honesty about sexual relations which was to be lost in the English novel till Lawrence.

The last Peril presents itself in the rambling, pointless story of plots and counterplots, mysteries within mysteries which arrange themselves around the battle of Culloden. Here are cheap laughs at lecherous ministers, oddly adjacent to Highland atrocities. This story was surely composed from the scraps of Hogg's notes for his *Jacobite Relics,* that collection of Highland songs which he had edited a few years before. It is also an obvious "filler" for the third volume, for its episodes are arbitrary in number, and at the end characters and mysteries are forgotten and unexplained. Some idea of the lack of unity of tone and control can be gathered by reading the comic opening, where much clowning takes place in a graveyard at night, with peasants amusing us with their superstitious fears and follies, and the beautiful Sally, the minister's housekeeper, the cynosure of lustful eyes. This farcical opening hardly accords with her end, after Culloden, on the desolate moorside, with

> Sally, left sitting, raving and singing her lullaby . . .
> beside the bodies of her murdered husband and
> former lover

or the consequent death of Sally and her baby.[27]

These three tales were fair game for adverse criticism. Wilson did the job with typical relish and a humorous tone which was supposed to mitigate offence. His review is worth attention, since it forms a turning point in Hogg's development, if we allow that *The Justified Sinner* was by now so far written that the effects of this review were to be found *after* that astonishing novel.[28] After all, two months before the last section of that novel had appeared as a trailer in *Blackwood's;* so that Wilson's words in that magazine could hardly alter it. They have profound implications for his work thereafter.

> We know not whether Hogg, the Well-Beloved, is greatest as a chivalrous or moral writer. In the one character, many prefer him to Scott; and, in the other, he is thought to beat Pope black and blue. His knights are wonderful creations of genius . . . and, as for his ladies, none more magnanimous ever followed a marching regiment.

These references to Charlie Scott and Musgrave of *The Three Perils of Man* and Clifford of *Basil Lee* are, of course, ironic, as we discover . . .

> It is indeed this rare union of high imagination with homely truth that constitutes the peculiar character of his writings. In one page, we listen to the song of the nightingale, and in another, to the grunt of the boar. Now the wood is vocal with the feathered choir; and then the sty bubbles and squeaks with a farm-sow, and a litter of nineteen pigwiggins. . . . Now enters bonnie Kilmeny, or Mary Lee, preparing to flee into Fairyland, or beat up the quarters of the Man in the Moon; and then, lo and behold, some huggered, red-armed, horny-fisted, glaur-nailed Girrzy. . . . It is impossible to foresee whether we are about to help ourselves to a pineapple or a fozey-turnip—to a golden pippin or a green crab—to noyau or castor oil—to white soup, syllabub and venison, or to sheep-head broth, haggis and hog's flesh. The table cloth, too, is damask . . . but villainously darned and washed in its own grease. . . .

Wilson then goes on to send up the first novel at great length, in the all too easy fashion of highlighting the most ridiculous parts. Hogg could not but fail to be influenced and hurt by the laughing stock position of his story. The effect would go all the deeper for Wilson's now high social and literary position, as editor of *Blackwood's* and, since 1820, Professor of Moral Philosophy at Edinburgh University, as well as being an accepted member of the "Lake" school of poets. By now it would be recognised that Wilson was the "heir apparent" to the monarchy of Scottish letters. His conclusion is one that Hogg could not ignore.

Now, James Hogg, Shepherd of Ettrick, and would-be author of the Chaldee Manuscript, and of the murder of Begbie, this style of writing will not by any means enable your pot to boil. . . . The public taste is not very refined, not over-delicate; but there are things innumerable in these three volumes, which the public will not bolt. You have no intention of being an immoral writer, and we aquit you of that; but you have an intention to be a most unmannerly writer. . . . You think you are showing your know-ledge of human nature, in these your coarse daubings, and that you are another Shakespeare. But consider that a writer may be indelicate, coarse, gross, even beastly, and yet not at all natural. We have heard such vulgarity objected to even in Glasgow; and it is not thought readable aloud at Largs. . . . Confound us if we ever saw in print anything at all resembling some of your female fancies; and if you go on at this rate, you will be called before the Kirk Session. This may be thought vigour by many of your friends in the Auld Town, and originality, and genius, and so forth; deal it out to them in full measure over the gin-jug, or even the tea-cup; but it will not do at a Public Entertainment. . . . You are worth twenty score of Stots and dogs . . . but you know little or nothing of the real powers and capacities of James Hogg, and would fain be the fine gentleman, the painter of manners, and the dissector of hearts. That will never do in this world. But only take our advice, and your books to come will make you a Cock-Laird. So let us see you at Ambrose's . . . and we will put you in the way of getting five hundred gold guineas. . . .

I have quoted at length because it seems to me that this review sums up the pressures on Hogg at this time to abandon his more ambitious plans in fiction and poetry. It also clearly positions him in a class or literary situation which stresses his being the Ettrick Shepherd, *Blackwood's* "man in the country" or even "tame shepherd." When Wilson says

In the Shepherd's verses there are occasional touches of good superstition; but his prose is good only on subjects of a very homely or vulgar nature . . .

he is almost drawing up a programme for Hogg's work after *The Justified Sinner*. Two pieces of evidence show how demoralised Hogg was to grow with continual blocking and criticism of his ventures. The first is from his 1832 autobiography, when he looks at his *The Three Perils of Man* with eyes embittered by *literati* criticism. From the fresh enthusiasm for his beloved tales of Michael Scott the wizard, now he sees it as something for which he must apologise, of which he sees the naive flaws—

Lord preserve me! What a medley I made of it!

135

> For I never in my life rewrote a page of prose . . .
> I dashed on and on, and mixed up with what might
> have been one of the best historical tales our country
> ever produced such a mass of diablerie as retarded
> the main story, and rendered the whole perfectly
> ludicrous . . . the next year I produced *The Three
> Perils of Women* . . . there is a good deal of pathos
> and absurdity in both the tales of this later work;
> but I was all this while writing as if in desperation,
> and see matters now in a different light.[29]

At this time (1832) he began to collect his work. It is
an indication of the shallowness of contemporary
criticism and of his own eventual lack of self-confidence
that he decided to savage *The Three Perils of Man*. He
cut it to one-third of its original length. He stripped
away all the magnificent folklore and colourful supernatural extravaganza, leaving merely the Border
skirmish which he called, for the purposes of the
collection, *The Siege of Roxburgh,* the only version
to be published till the restoration of the full original
in the 1972 edition.

But this was the climax of his misdirected development and disillusion. At the moment, with *The
Justified Sinner* well under way, Hogg had to soldier
on. The tone of insecurity and wistful hope that his
friends might help him emerges in a letter he wrote
to Scott expressing

> how anxious I was that you should glance over the
> proofs [of *The Three Perils of Man*], for I am
> grown to have no confidence whatsoever in my own
> taste or discernment in what is to be well or ill taken
> by the world or by individuals. Indeed it appears that
> were I to make my calculations by inverse proportion
> I would be oftener right than I am. . . .[30]

NOTES

1. *The Three Perils of Man*, ed. Douglas Gifford, 1972, p. i.
2. *The Three Perils of Man*, p. 2.
3. *The Three Perils of Man*, p. 2.
4. *The Three Perils of Man*, p. 5-6.
5. *The Three Perils of Man*, p. 75.
6. *The Three Perils of Man*, p. 97.
7. *The Three Perils of Man*, p. 141.
8. *The Three Perils of Man*, p. 174.
9. *The Three Perils of Man*, p. 201.
10. *The Three Perils of Man*, p. 230.
11. *The Three Perils of Man*, p. 231.
12. *The Three Perils of Man*, p. 232.
13. *The Three Perils of Man*, p. 284.
14. *The Three Perils of Man*, p. 288.
15. *The Three Perils of Man*, p. 396.
16. *Domestic Manners*, p. 70.
17. *Strout*, p. 243.
18. *The Three Perils of Women*, vol. I, p, 178.
19. *The Three Perils of Women*, vol. I, p. 197.
20. *The Three Perils of Women*, vol. I, p. 208.
21. *The Three Perils of Women* ,vol. I, p. 25.
22. *The Three Perils of Women*, vol. I, p. 22.
23. *The Three Perils of Women*, vol. II, p. 109.
24. *The Three Perils of Women*, vol. II, p. 112.
25. *The Three Perils of Man*, vol. II, p. 135.
26. *The Three Perils of Women*, vol. I, p. 101.
27. *The Three Perils of Women*, vol. III, p. 310.
28. *Blackwood's Magazine*, vol. XIV, 1823, pp. 427-437. It is worth noticing that this is the *amended* review, since Blackwood thought the original too strong! Cf. *Strout*, p. 253.
    Blackwood says "When I first read your terrible scraping of [Hogg] I enoyed it excessively; but on seeing it in types, I began to feel a little for the poor monster; and above all, when I considered it might perhaps irritate the creature as to drive him to some beastly personal attack on you, I thought it better to pause. . . ."
29. *Autobiography*, p. 459.
30. In a letter of November 16, 1821 to Walter Scott (unpublished) in the Blackwood Papers of the National Library of Scotland.

CHAPTER FIVE

THE PRIVATE MEMOIRS AND CONFESSIONS OF A JUSTIFIED SINNER (1824)

IF *The Three Perils of Man* is Hogg's most ambitious work, then *The Justified Sinner* is his finest. It is the culmination of years of development through trial and error, the natural fusion of all three strands of inspiration which, so far, he had kept apart. It is indisputably his work, since it relates back to themes in earlier stories which I have discussed, and forward to "miniatures" with exactly the same ambiguity in their treatment of the Devil like "The Brownie of the Black Haggs" (1828) or of the anti-hero as in *An Edinburgh Bailie* (1824).[1] If any final proof is needed that this is Hogg's work, let the doubtful read these and especially a story not included in Hogg's collected *Tales* of 1837, passed over by all his critics, but highly important in that it is an uncanny echo of the novel— "The Strange Letter of a Lunatic," in *Frasers Magazine,* 1830. Here is the meeting with the Devil in Edinburgh (on Castle Hill, this time), and the consequent torment caused by his adopting the hero's own likeness.

> Never was there a human creature in such a dilemma as I now found myself. I was conscious of possessing the same body and spirit that I ever did . . . but here was another being endowed with the same personal qualifications, who looked as I looked, thought as I thought, and expressed what I would have said . . . engaged in every transaction along with me. . . . I had become two bodies with one soul between them

. . . or, what I rather begin to suspect, the devil in my likeness.[2]

Can there be any doubt that the same man wrote this who had described the sinner as follows?

I was a being incomprehensible to myself. Either I had a second self, who transacted business in my likeness, or else my body was at times possessed by a spirit over which it had no control . . . I began to have secret terrors that the great enemy of man's salvation was exercising powers over me. . . . And yet to shake him off was impossible—we were incorporated together—identified with one another. . . .[3]

There is also exactly the same ambiguity of interpretation, since the short story ends with a piece of objective evidence (like part three in the novel) that the "lunatic" may not be so; that the rational and the supernatural explanations exist in ambiguity together.

But it is surely now unnecessary to argue the case for Hogg's authorship, although I do think it most probable that Hogg, at this point on the best of terms with John Gibson Lockhart, having dedicated his last novel to him, might well have discussed his story and structure with a fellow-writer of fiction whose *Matthew Wald,* the study of a lunatic, was in preparation at the same time, and came out in 1824 also. If so, such discussion must be the only example of fruitful interchange of ideas between the Edinburgh *literati* and Hogg in terms of his fiction. It is also probable that the crucial "trick" basis of the novel, the deliberate creation of the dual interpretation, was generated in the company of Lockhart, who had already, in the infamous matter of "The Chaldee Manuscript," joined with Hogg and Wilson in literary practical joke. The letter of "August 1823," in the third part of the novel, signed "James Hogg" really did appear in *Blackwood's Magazine* then, and the novel's editor refers to the frequent hoaxes of that magazine.[4]

But even if these are signs of Lockhart's advice or help with plot and structure, there is ultimately no need to belittle Hogg's own superb achievement. Nevertheless one can understand how it occurred when it did more fully by briefly scanning its literary surroundings; in Scotland, in the European Gothic tradition, and finally in terms of Hogg himself.

In Scotland Hogg would find much to stimulate his theme. Burns's *Holy Willie's Prayer* (1785) and Scott's *Heart of Midlothian* (1818) could (although I am by no means insisting that they did) offer him his central bigoted Presbyterian and his Edinburgh setting, respectively. Scott's novel has a mysterious devil-figure in George Staunton, has much drama expressed in diabolic metaphor taking place near Nicol Muschet's cairn and Arthur's Seat, and is also much concerned with family division, with two very different sisters and the matter of the strict religious conscience of David Deans at its heart. Beyond this there is the thematically related work of Lockhart, and of Galt, whose study of greedy, fanatically obsessive Claud Walkinshaw in *The Entail* was to appear in the same year as Hogg's work. Hogg would certainly have read Galt's *The Provost* (1822), where a canny, self-interested, self-justifying and hardly heroic central figure reveals his motivation and achievement through a dramatic monologue not dissimilar to Robert Wringhim's.

Beyond the strictly literary tradition there is much more that could have aided Hogg's vision. Louis Simpson admirably traced Hogg's possible debt to antinomian ministers of the past in his own Borders, men like Thomas Boston and James Hog, who had in the early eighteenth century fought for and written on "the Auchterarder Creed," "who held that salvation was not contingent upon faith, *et cetera,* but was the effect of justification, of grace."[5] He also argues convincingly that Hogg was working close to real life. *The Confession, Etc. of Nicol Muschet of Boghal,* hanged as a murderer at the Grassmarket in 1721, was reprinted in Edinburgh in 1818. Here is that paradoxical, weird tone of justification for atrocity in the criminal's postulating satanic temptation, with that horrifying note of exultation in being God's agent, as Muschet concludes

What shall I say of God's free grace and mercy! . . . But very oft of the rudest piece of clay, that most excellent potter makes vessels of honour, the more to manifest his singular power and art.[6]

And, long before, G. H. Millar had pointed out the similarity between the kind of anecdotes of the supernatural showing God's Providence told by the minister Robert Wodrow in his *Analecta* and Hogg's tale.[7] Hogg knew the work of many major theologians like Wodrow and Sinclair in *Satan's Invisible World Discovered* (1685), and doubtless they left an imprint in his imagination.

I have already argued that Hogg should not be thought of as a Gothic novelist in any fundamental sense. His roots are in the Borders and Scotland, and his Devil is basically the same Devil as in *The Three Perils of Man,* though more subtle and elusive, while the situation is that of the Ballad "The Daemon Lover." Nevertheless Hogg would be aware of the public taste for the horrible and marvellous since *The Castle of Otranto* (1764) by Walpole, (which he read with pleasure), Godwin's *Caleb Williams* (1794), Lewis's *The Monk* (1796), Mrs Radcliffe's *The Italian* (1797), Hoffman's *Elixiere des Teufels* (1815-16), Mary Shelley's *Frankenstein* (1818), and Charles Maturin's *Melmoth the Wanderer* (1820). All or any of these, with their love-hate relationships, satanic visitors, religious egotisms, and confessional horrors, may have caught Hogg's attention as he looked around for new models after the failure of his other types of fiction. But given Hogg's eclectic and undiscriminating eye one can never be sure what it was that sparked him off. It could have been anything from Marlowe's *Faust* to the contrast between Blifil and Tom in *Tom Jones*.

But one need not look as far back in time or abroad to Gothic fiction of the day to find the most forceful stimulus to Hogg's imagination. I have already argued that a recurrent theme began to emerge in Hogg's fiction as early as *The Spy* stories and *The Long Pack*. Dark, inscrutable forces surround and trap a poor innocent in a web so intricate and vast that it is far beyond his ability to see the true nature of his persecutors or their power. It is not too far-fetched to see here an objectification of his own situation, since we know that he felt from the *Spy* days onwards that there was a consipracy of the gentry against him; that his relationship with those black-clad "devils," the young advocates who diabolically altered his draft of "The Chaldee Manuscript," was very much a love-hate affair; that towards the end of his career he became obsessive about the way in which even "friends" like Wilson and publishers like Blackwood were exploiting and abusing his name and placing deliberate obstacles in the way of his publishing the novels and stories that would re-establish his greatness as a writer.

We are indebted to Barbara Bloedé for identifying

the connection between Hogg's unsureness of identity, fear of his *literati* contemporaries, and *The Justified Sinner*. Tracing back the possibility of personal insecurity to his earliest days, when his impoverished family had to "reject" him at the age of six to work away from family and school, she provides a solid basis for seeing Hogg as one who could express with bitter familiarity Robert Wringhim's feelings of exclusion and uncertainty. She rightly stresses the damage that must have been done to Hogg when, after whole-heartedly trusting Wilson, he found that it was Wilson who was guilty of the "beastly depravity" of the attack on his *Mountain Bard* in *Blackwood's* of 1821. From 1822 the "Noctes Ambrosianae" series in that magazine actually created an *alter ego* for Hogg, with Wilson's picture of him as the irresponsible drinking buffoon, which London found to be so inappropriate when Hogg went there in 1832.

> In these circumstances we can see *The Confessions* as something more than satire; it is the exteriorisation of Hogg's own conflicts and a projection of those unconscious feelings of guilt and unworthiness. Its force derives from there; it was the most personal thing he was ever to write, and it must have helped him preserve his sanity in what was one of the most painful periods of a far from easy life.[8]

If the subject-matter was naturally within Hogg, the techniques and background knowledge of theology and Bible were there too. The knowledge had already produced a novel sympathising with the extreme Presbyterians of the seventeenth century, and would frequently again produce stories like "The Cameronian Preacher's Tale" which would employ his superb ear for the varying registers of religious language from the dignified and sonorous to the bigoted and hysterical. Ian Campbell has fully analysed how Hogg puts such unique ability to a use in *The Justified Sinner* which the reader of Hogg's time would appreciate much more readily for its profound nuance and subtle implication than we can now.[8]

At this point the tracing of influences and precedents must stop. Hogg's novel is unique in its concrete, vivid imagery, its dramatic and bold action, its terse style and its peculiarly Scottish irony. All these are charteristics of his earlier work, and it is time we stopped being surprised that a shepherd wrote like this and understood that it was because he was a shepherd that he wrote like this.

There is one aspect of his novel that is crucial, and has been neglected. It is quite deliberately ambiguous in a way which gives dramatic shape to the novel, as well as two mutually exclusive interpretations which move together in a way which echoes the *doppelganger* theme of the story. Always there are the two possibilities. The Devil and the other supernatural apparitions may not exist at all, and may merely be a link with creatures of a diseased mind; or they may be the very real instruments of punishment and damnation of a great sinner. Indeed, the very last sentences of the novel point the reader towards these twin responses.

In short, we must either conceive him not only the greatest fool, but the greatest wretch, on whom was ever stamped the form of humanity—[this allowing that the sinner awakened God's wrath and a *real* devil]—*or* [my emphasis] that he was a religious maniac, who wrote and wrote about a deluded creature, till he arrived at that height of madness. . . .[9]

144

It is a brilliant and creative sleight of hand which was, I believe, deliberately intended to anticipate and disarm the kind of criticism to which Hogg had grown all too accustomed. To the critic who would censure the novel on, say, the score of "diablerie and nonsense" it could be argued that the story was the psychological study of a religious fanatic who became a lunatic. Conversely, were the novel to be attacked as being a morbid and distasteful study of an anti-heroic Basil Lee-type of figure, Hogg could reply that his tale, drawn from tradition and legend, as he stresses from the opening, was akin to those country tales of the supernatural which he had collected for *Winter Evening Tales,* a kind of diabolic *Pilgrim's Progress.*

All this gives the novel its very structure, one of its great strengths. The *parts* of the novel (three of them: Editor's narrative, Memoirs and Confessions of the sinner, and Editor's comments at the end) and the arrangement of characters and incidents within the parts are designed so that they fit an overall pattern of rational/objective experience set against supernatural/subjective experience. This is not a total separation—but broadly one can argue that in part one the rational mind of reader *and* writer struggles to impose a logical explanation for the events therein; while in part two the reader tends, temporarily at least, to allow himself to be carried by the subjective account of supernatural events. Part three is a weighing-up of the two claims, with new evidence on both sides, which significantly comes to no final resolution of both or decision for either.

Even the tone of parts one and two is deliberately contrasted. The first has a sensible manner, referring to tradition and records, citing court debate as circumstantial evidence (a standard Hogg device for making the incredible more palatable), telling the story from the same stance as *The Brownie of Bodsbeck,* with "values" implied which are to be seen as "normal" and humane. The second reverses this, substituting the abnormal, anti-heroic, and confessedly mean and petty, with the former humane standards intruding *via* figures like Blanchard, the kindly minister, and the earthy, compassionate jailer. The natural has become unnatural; recto has given way to verso, white to black.

And *within* each part there are sub-sets of the total pattern. There can be no doubt that Hogg intended his two branches of Dalcastle relationships to form positive and negative "congruent triangles." The Laird of Dalcastle, natural, Wat of Chapelhope-like simple Scot of the old school who tolerates extreme believers but likes his drink and his blether is meant to be set against the Reverend Wringhim, utterly the opposite in his joyless devotions. Further, there is the irony that the Laird's "rape" of his wife, while it demonstrates that the man is far from perfect, and even if it seems unnatural, is nothing like as unnatural as the hypocrisy on Wringhim's part which allows him to father Robert during a night's "devotions."

At the next corner of the triangle are the two ladies; similarly opposed in that one is humane, warm and compassionate, while the other is "the most severe and gloomy of all bigots to the principles of the reformation." But, as with the two "fathers," the irony lies in the fact that the love is found in Arabella, the Laird's mistress, a "fat, bouncing dame" of easy virtue, jolly, and "as much attached to George as if he had been her own son." Lady Dalcastle may repudiate her natural child, but the socially unnatural lady does not, just as in *Basil Lee* Clifford the prostitute gave charity when it seemed neither due nor likely.

146

Moreover, this mistress together with Bell Calvert the prostitute becomes the force for Good and sanity after the Laird's death.

The main opposition of the three is that of George and Robert. This needs little comment, being so fully developed, but there are nice touches in Hogg's making Robert the scholar, good at the "arid" disciplines of grammar, maths and theology, while George is a poor scholar, but has a social, natural grace that his bastard brother lacks.[10] (Hogg thought bastards unnatural in much more than the fact of their birth, as his tale "Sandy Elshinder" shows.)

Does Hogg possibly approach symbolism of the kind that Scott uses in examples of blood relations like Rob Roy and Nicol Jarvie, who in one sense stand for much deeper divisions within Scotland? Or like Stevenson's divided family in *The Master of Ballantrae* (1889), where the two very different brothers and their immediate family represent a sick division endemic within the Scottish mind? I think he does. For once he developed the more casual oppositions of earlier work like that of Wat of Chapelhope and Claverhouse, or the friar and Michael Scott and created them with a larger significance, so that the Dalcastle-Wringhim division symbolises not just a Scottish healthy tradition of wholeness set against a spiritual Deformation which is a result of the more morbid developments of the Reformation, but a universal statement expressing itself in human metaphors which clearly argues the same case as Scott's symbolic Jeannie Deans for instinctive, natural, spontaneous Goodness as opposed to tortuous and self-destructive attempts to base morality and religion on dogma or false logic.

Having established his white and black pattern Hogg moves quickly into his sensational narrative. Almost

147

immediately the alert reader will begin to wonder in which of two ways he should respond to the events. On one hand he can, when the action seems incredible, as when supernatural events are witnessed by many bystanders, maintain a rational interpretation by stressing Hogg's deliberate repetition on the first page of *tradition*. Thus the marvellous events may simply be ascribed to superstitious tradition, and the rational reader will simply "subtract" them to get at the residual true and explicable events of a lunatic bigot who systematically destroyed his hated family till his madness in turn destroyed him.

But the reader may also read in a fundamentally different way, with a suspension of disbelief or even a traditional religious viewpoint and experience something fundamentally, morally and aesthetically different. Because of this I intend to separate these two interpretations. Let us look at the Editor's narrative first.

On a rational reading the central figure, Robert, is the son of a crazy minister, a hypocrite who achieves his sexual desires in the same way as the curate in *The Brownie of Bodsbeck* sought to, in hysterical religious fervour which gives way at its peak to unremembered indulgence. The son is a Basil Lee with a greater degree of mental instability, and a terribly warping set of background influences. He is, as the early tennis matches reveal, a masochist, bleeding pathetically and unheroically from his nose, pursuing a martyrdom which is sick, and uttering curses, with the help of his equally warped father, which are direct tokens of their stage of mental illness —the greater the curse, the more advanced the illness. There is the further bitter but quite logical irony that Robert, father and mother take great pride in each aspect of their sickness, be it their pride, guilt or sexual frigidity.

Hogg is at great pains to safeguard the possibility of this level of interpretation. There need be no devils at the tennis matches, however black Robert may look; and one episode in this part illustrates perfectly Hogg's desire to run with the rational hares as well as hunt with supernatural hounds. Robert eventually, in his growing madness has convinced himself, by way of his imagined friend, that George must die—this we learn from his later account. In part one we see the murder attempt from the outside, and very weird it seems to be. It is the biggest strain so far on our credulity, so Hogg balances the apparently supernatural appearance of the colossal apparition in Robert's likeness, which George sees as a spirit, with an extended discussion about refraction and "the man of science's" delight in appreciating the logical explanation behind the marvellous phenomenon. Words like "phenomenon," "refracted," "science," "sublunary," "terrestrial" are used in this rather indigestible preamble to the apparition because Hogg wants nineteenth-century rationalism to walk alongside, but not holding hands with, a credulous acceptance of supernatural happening. (Hogg will later use the same phenomenon of refraction creating "apparitions" in the poem "A Real Vision" in 1830, and in the article "Nature's Magic Lantern" in the collected *Tales* of 1837.)

There is a final apparent obstacle to a rational interpretation of the Editor's narrative. Bell Calvert, in giving evidence to Arabella Logan about the death of George, identifies a mysterious accomplice of Robert's, who takes a major part in George's murder, who is very like but definitely not the suspected Drummond.

149

Shortly after, the two ladies together see this accomplice, who signals to them, and causes Arabella to faint because he looks like the murdered George. Here we seem to have objective evidence that there is a companion to Robert who is *not* just a figment of his mind, but at the very least is real, and whose abilities in face-changing seem supernatural.

One need not invoke L. L. Lee's important stress on Hogg's "envelope" of tradition at the beginning and end of the Editor's account to dispel the importance of this "objective" evidence.[11] There is a perfectly reasonable and psychologically satisfying way of reading these two episodes. In the first, we remember that Bell Calvert had been under great stress ("I had been abandoned in York by an artful and consummate fiend"), had been drinking, was greatly taken with Drummond, who left. Add to this that all she saw took place in moonlight, and the total of what she tells that would be acceptable to a court of law is that Drummond did not kill George, and that Robert had an accomplice. And in the second, there are specific indications planted by Hogg to make us question the reliability of these ladies' testimony. Only after much prompting by Mrs Logan does Bell "remember" that Robert's companion reminds her of George. Their imaginations are described as "heated"—and what would be more likely than that poor, grief-crazed Arabella Logan, brooding over George's murder by Robert, should create the victim's face before her, and that her ally, Bell, should catch this hysterical impression from her? Slyly Hogg emphasises just this, when he describes the infectious mood; Bell Calvert asks

"Yet, if it is not he, [George] who can it be?"

"It *is* he!" cried Mrs Logan, hysterically.

"Yes, yes, it *is* he!" cried the landlady, in unison.

"It is who?" said Mrs Calvert. "Whom do you mean, mistress?"

"Oh, I don't know! I don't know! I was affrighted."

. . . Mrs Calvert turned the latter . . . out of the apartment, observing that there seemed to be some infection in the air of the room. . . .[12]

Grief has become hysteria. One can well imagine that the episode would gather a strange significance in the re-telling of the landlady, for example; so that the mass hysteria would be the legendary part of "all with which history, justiciary records, and tradition" furnished the Editor, as he looks back from 1823-4 on the events of 1687-1712.

But the novel is two stories, and the first part has more and richer ironies to offer if we read it as an external glimpse of the Devil entering into a "Game of Souls." Much of what is happening now will have to wait for Robert's account to appear clearly, but it should be noted that Hogg stresses Robert's prayer-curses against the Laird's side of the family. This is the characteristic folk-tale condition which opens so many stories of retribution of Hogg's. The Devil has been awakened, and appears at the tennis matches. The language describing this bears the sly hallmark of Hogg's treatment of these strange situations. On one level the references to devils and devilish/sinister/infernal/damnable situations is acceptable as colloquial and racy metaphor—but on a second level it is meant to be taken absolutely literally. The "devilish-looking youth" of "malignant" eye who keeps steadfastly "to his old joke of damnation" is Hogg's traditional way of telling us that the Devil is present. Notice too the emphasis on position—"hellish-looking" Robert appears at his brother's right hand, "always within a few yards of him, generally the same distance . . . darting looks at him that chilled his soul." George is ostracised, as his friends fear a "sinister" design, and even though he tells no one of his actions, there, always in the same spatial relationship, will appear his brother, or "a friend of more malignant aspect . . . in the form of his brother."

The reason that the *place* of Robert's appearance must be stressed is that it demonstrates the efficacy of the curse which Robert tells us he and his father pronounced on George after George's rudeness ("Mercy be about us, Sir! Is this the crazy minister's son from Glasgow?") which announced Robert's bastardy to the world—as well as insulting the reverend Wringhim. The Devil is brought into real power in the story by their curse:

> Set thou the wicked over him
> *And upon his right hand*
> *Give thou his greatest enemy*
> *Even Satan, leave to stand.*[13]

Satan will do more than stand. But his presence, undeniable, raises a problem. How do we account for the fact that Robert recalls being at the tennis matches? The answer establishes a crucial aspect concerning the Devil's power. Robert, described as *more* malignant or fanatic than usual, is in fact *possessed*. The Devil can share Robert's conscious mind. We can therefore meet Robert, Robert *and* the Devil, the Devil *as* Robert—and the Devil as any of these as well as staging diversions elsewhere. Stories in the later *Shepherd's Calendar* make it quite clear that all these modes of activity are within the "rules" for the Devil's part in the attempt to win souls. Thus the Devil can appear as Drummond, as George, as well as being within Robert. Once we are in tune with Hogg's idiom here it is easy to appreciate the sinister implications of that "stranger" who told George about Robert's presence at the tennis match. Such "strangers" and "someones" are key clues in Hogg's supernatural method. This "someone" will fortuitously cry "A plot! A plot! Treason . . . down with the bloody incendiaries at the Black Bull" against George; will create that "mysterious temporary madness" which grips Wringhim senior and his Whig friends at this time. The technique reaches its sly best when Hogg tells us that no mob, no whippers-up of the clash, can be found, and "the devil an enemy had they to pursue"! The sinister mob has vanished "like so many thousands of phantoms! "[14]

There are two major incidents remaining in part one which deserve attention in their supernatural aspects. The first is the murder attempt at Arthur's Seat, and the second the actual murder. In the first, there is again the emphasis on the fact that George sees the horrifying apparition of his brother when he turns his eyes *to the right*. There's a slight clash between the two interpretations here, since it's hardly likely that the arrogant striding apparition is a reflection of the cringing, crouching real Robert behind George. One presumes that the Devil ceases to possess Robert immediately before the actual attempt, since it will emerge as vital to the Devil's plans that Robert make his own free choice and do his own evil deeds. Robert is then like a puppet with its wires cut, reduced from his inflated power to his sneaking hypocrisy. He even tells George that his friend came with (that is, *within*) him to the hillfoot, but left him there (to appear in apparition to George).

After this failure follows another curse, invoking the help of "the Lord" "to destroy and root out" the Dalcastles. Murder has been invoked for the first time, and Satan's powers will be correspondingly increased.

The actual murder introduces another device of Hogg's—that of letting the Devil speak absolute truth, but in a context which will achieve the effect of a lie. Thus the Devil's insults, apparently to George, about being a braggart, a blot on nature, and his threats to have his soul are in fact to Robert. The technique will be superb in part two, but it achieves rare effect when the Devil exults with complete honesty after the murder:

"Ah, hell has it!   my friend, my friend! "[15]

To help him from the scene of the crime Robert is possessed, Hogg taking care to describe his "very peculiar" gait. "He walked as if he had been flat soled, and his legs made of steel, without any joints in his feet or ankles" captures the zombie-like movement of one whose mind is not completely his own.

After this murder Robert is almost totally the Devil's. Almost—for the Devil needs yet to make Robert commit "that act for which, according to the tenets he embraced, there was no remission," the act of suicide. The Devil's power is great now, and he hardly deigns to hide, but signals to the ladies to overhear Robert accepting his own creed of predestination. Arabella remarks that Robert is possessed, that his breath is of the charnel house and realises that Gilmartin is imitating George to deepen Robert's guilt. She tells us that the Almighty will subvert nature to punish a fratricide of all crimes.

In all this a pattern of power has emerged. The Devil's ability waxes and wanes according to how much rope he is given, and can only gain entrance through guilt. Thus when George is mean, and delivers his nasty insult to Robert, he exposes himself, and the curse which follows takes effect. When George neglects true religion, watching girls in church, he consequently draws "fiendish glances" upon himself. His ultimate downfall comes, significantly, as a result of his frequenting stews and taverns.

The pattern works in George's favour fairly enough. When he generously vows to befriend Robert "it was a good while before his gratuitous attendant appeared at his side again. . . ." The outstanding example of this is in the otherwise irrelevant, if vivid, extended description of George's unwillingness to deface the "fairy web" of dew which garnishes his hat as he walks on that serene morning past Saint Anthony's chapel, "light of heart." The scene is meant to establish the fact that George is in a state of grace and harmony with nature. He has acted generously, and there are powers, unspecified but good, working on his behalf that morning. Robert's account will tell of these later. It suffices for this part that the pattern is shown to have Good within its shape, that the battle is seen to be between the Devil and God.

* * *

In looking at the two interpretations of the second part it is convenient to identify three phases of development in Robert's situation. The stages are identifiable in both readings, but of course they mark off very different kinds of experience in each.

First there is Robert's boyhood. Although there is little complexity here, nevertheless two responses are possible. We can either see this as supplying the material necessary for us to understand Robert's conditioning so that we bring a "modern" consciousness to bear on his account, and read it as the process that warps his psychology; or we can read it as an account of sin and the revelation of the breeding-ground of Evil that will grow monstrously thereafter.

The second phase is entered with Robert's "exaltation," when he has the experience of transcendence and the meeting with the stranger. From this point on the question of real Devil or madness is paramount. From now on we have parallels with part one, with a distortion that makes vices into virtues, and there will be a much greater burden of conjecture for the reader to bear.

The curse of the Reverend Wringhim after Robert's release from jail takes Robert into the third phase of his madness, or conjures the Devil to even greater atrocities. Either way, destruction of Robert's personality terminates this.

Once again, for a full appreciation of Hogg's ironic skill in creating a totally ambiguous design, it is necessary to read this part as two accounts. Let us firstly read it as the account of an insane person. Not only does Robert suffer enormous pressures as he grows up with the problem of his paternity, since either he is the Laird's unacknowledged son or he is a bastard (either belief bound to cause him immense personal turmoil), but he is additionally reared in terms of a religion which is one of hate rather than love. One can only speculate as to the destructive effect on a young mind to be told that, as he is not yet one of the Elect, he is damned—and told so by his father-figure.

I have *struggled* with the Almighty *long and hard*

156

> . . . but have as yet no certain token of his [Robert's] acceptance . . . I have indeed *fought a hard fight,* but have been *repulsed* . . . although I have cited his words *against him,* and *endeavoured* to hold him at his promise, he hath so many *turnings* in the supremacy of his power that I have been *rejected* [my emphases].[16]

It is worth noting the cleverness of speeches like this. Not only will there be an ironic comment available when we look at the supernatural interpretation, since "turnings" suggests the serpent image of Satan, but also in the psychological interpretation we are made aware that the God implied here is the product of a sick mind who sees religion in terms of a structure of hate, with a God like that of Holy Willie at its apex. No wonder Robert will graduate as "sword, scourge, and terror" of all those who were not subjected to childhood experience as hate-filled as his.

Poor Robert could not have been more effectively brainwashed by the most sophisticated of modern methods. The pressure is utterly unremitting. However much he prays, paradoxically, like Stephen Dedalus at his most devout, he discovers even more sins. It is a *Catch-22* situation, with the nett result that Robert

> got into great confusion relating to my sins and repentances and knew neither where to begin nor how to proceed. . . .[17]

Add to this the burden of original sin, and the picture of a terrified child becomes as appalling as Joyce's. Only Joyce in *The Portrait of the Artist as a Young Man* has a comparable analysis of the terrible effect of a child's mind of such complete, imaginatively powerful and devastating mythology, and only Joyce conjures up such a compelling picture of the cruel God which exists within the young mind. Robert, like Stephen, is a sensitive child, it is stressed, intelligent and vulnerable. It is fascinating to compare Joyce's crucial chapter on Stephen's release, which ends in "profane joy," with Stephen reconciled to the Earth and reborn by the sea, with the very similar crisis point for Robert, with its very different outcome. Where Stephen's experience is cathartic, Robert's "release" is too late. Priding himself on his sexual frigidity, moving always in on himself, Robert's only "release" from his horror is to go mad, and instead of experiencing epiphany which reconciles him to the earthly, Robert's mind *separates* him from the earthly.

> An exaltation of spirit lifted me, as it were, far above the earth and the sinful creatures crawling on its surface; and I deemed myself as an eagle among the children of men, soaring on high, and looking down with pity and contempt on the grovelling creatures below.[18]

The sequel bears comparison with Joyce too, for instead of meeting an earthly creature, symbol of mortal and profane beauty, an angel of life, like Stephen, Robert reaches into the interior of his mind and *creates* the figure who will then be able to offer him relief from repression of the desires which his faith sees as evil. His father's declaration of Election has come as too swift an unwinding of the over-taut mind, and the spring has broken. Is it an accident that the name he gives his friend is an echo of that childhood arch-enemy, McGill?

Robert, now in the second phase of his psychological disintegration, creates a personified objectification of his repressed desires. Gilmartin relieves Robert of his loneliness, and allows outlets for his greed, pent-up hate, and — eventually — lust. Understandably enough it will be he who suggests the morally suspect courses of action, since that will relieve Robert of responsibility. Of course he resembles Robert, since, in a very real way, he *is* Robert. And of course Robert will have strange feelings which he uses the metaphor of "enchantment" to express, since these will be the psychosomatic accompaniments of going mad. And of course the stranger will say that he has come to be a disciple of Robert's, thus supplying much-needed flattery and sense of ego, although later this relationship will alter to take account of the atrocities committed, and Gilmartin will begin to seem a tempter to Robert, since only in this way will his burden of guilt be transferred. Thus too Gilmartin knows Robert's thoughts, and of course stresses the dominating fear in Robert's mind, that pre-occupation with the validity of justification by faith rather than works.

How cleverly Hogg picks language which permits this and another reading! When Robert feels a "deliverance" from Gilmartin on leaving him, the term can refer to the relief felt after the passing of a kind of mental seizure—or to Christian and real deliverance from evil. When he sees his father's eyes burning like candles, the significance of the metaphor may be that the mad boy projects his inner intensity on to his similarly mad father—or the images can carry an association of hellish heat.

The psychological damage is reinforced now as Wringhim senior dedicates the mad boy to God as a sword and scourge. Any chance of easing the child back down from his demented plane is destroyed, and Robert's ego now becomes prey to his id, his physical appearance begins to deteriorate in keeping with his mental illness, and the honesty of his account lessens acutely. We need increasingly to "read through" his account to the truth, as the "disciple" shifts to become his "guide and director," although with the residual cunning common to such cases he resolves at this point not to tell his parents about this friend. And the bouts develop, with obsession giving way to relief, bodily wasting and bitter tears marking the internal struggle.

There is at this point the problem that "several people" tell his parents he is in company with this friend, but cleverly Hogg provides the qualification— "they, at the same time, had all described him differently." Perhaps Robert *is* keeping bad company, but inventing his friend as scapegoat thereafter. He is by now not a reliable witness. The irony is that the greater Robert's guilt in these transgressions, the greater his *alter ego* has to become to stand as a plausible tempter. The final irony will emerge as Robert, deep in guilt, begins to *hint* to us, without ever being explicit, for he wishes the situation to be ambiguous, that this tempter *may* be suspect, a force for evil. The nearest he gets to this is when he questions whether he should bless the day of his Election or not, but the implied meaning is clear. If the Devil gives a poor mortal his exclusive attention, is that mortal not entitled to claim diminished responsibility, much as poor Nicol Muschet did in real life?

Looked at in this rational light, assuming that Robert is mad, key events in this part take on a clearer significance. One can even question whether the events Robert describes take place at all, like the Blanchard murder. Probably it does, but even then Robert's account is ambiguous. Gilmartin does not like Blanchard, and as Gilmartin watches him Gilmartin's face changes to resemble Blanchard's. What is really happening is that as the strong-willed old minister destroys Gilmartin/Robert's argument, so Gilmartin as representative of Robert's new self-confidence disappears. Naturally when Blanchard goes the *alter ego* demands the removal of his threat to its existence. We note that the last straw which decides Blanchard's murder is that he maintains that "it was every man's own blame if he was not saved"— that is, he asserts Justification by Works or good actions, that system of redemption which is anathema to Robert.

Robert is now very seriously ill, since he begins to have auxiliary hallucinations, as in his imagining that golden weapons are let down from the sky with their points to him. His mind creates a symbolism which at once expresses his guilt feelings, reflects his avarice and pride (they are both gold to be coveted as Robert covets the Dalcastle fortunes and a sign of his importance in the scheme of things). At the same time the hallucination provides further release, since the *alter ego* in its light re-defines Robert's goals, revealing to him even deeper repressed desires yet taking on the guilt that follows their indulgence.

Any hopes that a comparison of the tennis match accounts of part one and part two will shed light on each other are quickly lost. The only "fact" that emerges from comparison is one about Robert's mind. He is now creating his own version of reality where all is malleable for his gratification and consolation. Robert projects "terror and astonishment" on the episode which in the account of the first part consisted of his interruption of the game, George's accidental knocking him down, the fight that follows, and George's apology. Robert's account reveals his hysteria and his masochism ("none of them had the heart to kick him, although it appeared the only thing he wanted") and his ability to believe in a reality of his own:

Again I strode into the midst of them, and, eyeing them with threatening looks, they were so much confounded that they abandoned their sinful pastime, and fled everyone to his house! [19]

Jeering followers of his actions become "Christians" who share his triumph, and no mention is made of George's apology, while his own bloody nose and physical besting are forgotten.

One typical Hogg device ends this phase of his madness. Just as the first phase used old Barnet as a representative in the Wat of Chapelhope and Charlie Scott tradition of healthy human instinct for sense and compassion, so now the very jailer of Robert's prison suddenly shines through the tormented account to remind us that this lunatic is a "callant," a poor adolescent to be pitied, however sick and dangerous he may be. It is the jailer who tries to help him get in touch with relatives, and his action and words cut through and reduce the inflated egotism.

With that "strange distemper" whereby Robert conceives of himself as two people, Robert enters the third and terminal stage of madness. His disease begins to erode his sense of identity, since

I rarely conceived myself to be any of the two persons. I thought for the most part that my companion was one of them, and my brother the other. . . .[20]

What would be more likely than that these two most important aspects of Robert's life, himself as he would like to be in release, and the embodiment of everything

162

he wishes removed from his world, should dominate his mind?

His time sense also begins to collapse, and he loses that former control over his "relationship" with his *alter ego,* in that instead of keeping the communication private, or fairly so, he now believes that outsiders share his unnatural experiences. Moreover, he has by now shifted into being the servant of Gilmartin, rather than his disciple.

The Arthur's Seat episode is completely falsified, to the extent that where George accidentally knocked Robert down, now in this version Robert dashes himself furiously on George. Where he begged forgiveness and made promises, he now says, "though I do not recollect the circumstances of that deadly struggle very minutely, I know that I vanquished him so far as to force him to ask my pardon." Robert is incapable of truth now. Conscience gives a residual flicker now and again, as with the "white lady," a hallucinatory expression of guilt, but all the old symptoms are much more pronounced, like the wild swings from hysteria to inertia, as he runs to St Anthony's chapel, then stops dead to consider the awful actuality of what he intends. He even creates a power he does not have, by interpreting the death of the judge who decided for George as divine retribution occasioned by his friend. When he does kill George it is understandably on an occasion when George's actions have aroused intense sexual jealousy in addition to the hate he already feels—and his mind deliberately becomes vague as to the details of the murder, although his *alter ego* rejoices.

Spells of complete amnesia illustrate that he is approaching the final mental disintegration, with four months and three days cut down to thirty days, in a fashion that allows complete licence for all his dammed up sexuality, desire to drink, and greed. He comes to wearing the gaudy clothes of his excesses. Lawyer Clinkum and the lady may, according to Robert, "see" his *alter ego*—but can Robert's account be trusted at all now? And, taken as the last stages in delirium, one need not like Gide find these closing stages too demonological, since by this time Robert *must* externalise his massive guilt, not only making Gilmartin an obvious tempter, and, like Dorian Gray's picture, exemplifying Robert's horrid guilt in his distorted George-resembling face, but finding even more nightmarish creatures to express the degenerated id. He likes listening to the Cameronian Penpunt's tales of temptations and Devil visitation now, because such stories (apart from reflecting Robert's nature in the parallel sick love of the Auchtermuchty folk for their own picture of themselves as "damned") consolidate his view of himself as sorely tempted, an innocent who has been trapped. Like many in his condition, he even now has "lucid intervals" where he horribly perceives his own degeneration, glimpsing in the good woman who impresses him with the "simplicity of human nature" an insight into balanced and healthy mentality.

The closing scenes of crimson-pawed monsters are the end for poor Robert's over-heated mind. He is thrown out of lodgings for raving, his wasted body mirrored in his *alter ego*. And looking back over his decline, we now understand the curious love-hate relationship between them, Robert of course infatuated with his means of release from repression; while the hate aspect had of necessity to follow, since the love was for the personification of the expression of *unfulfilled* desires, and satiation following, hate then attached itself to the same expression.

*   *   *

In many ways the supernatural interpretation of part two is even more rich and satisfying than the profound and chilling modernity of the psychological reading. It employs a religious symbolism and a depth of irony unparallelled anywhere in Hogg.

In this interpretation the three "phases" useful in the last disappear as markers of *internal* change in Robert, and become markers to the stages of real demonic possession. The first demonstrates Robert's boyhood *sins,* the emphasis falling differently from before, explaining why the Devil picked him. He is a bastard, and Hogg's later tale of "Sandy Elshinder" shows that Hogg genuinely believed such to be morally suspect, people of talent but dangerous. Robert is "third in a direct line who had all been children of adultery; and it was well-known that all such were born half-deils themselves, and nothing was more likely than that they should hold intercourse with their fellows." As Barnaby the shepherd boy told us in "The Woolgatherer," there are very strict and traditional folk-rules to the Devil's game, whereby the Devil can only gain entrance where the door has been left open for him; "the de'il and his adgents, they fash nane but the good fowk, the cameronians and the praying ministers."[21] Robert may be an insignificant fellow in terms of earthly show, but in spiritual pride, sin, and especially his habit of lying he is of course a supreme challenge to the Father of Lies. The first part moreover shows him to be hypocritical, mean, sadistic and ungrateful, as well as cowardly. He may be tormented by fear of sin, but his torment is selfish, since beyond the actual fear he is as amoral as Merodach, the Brownie of the Black Haggs (or his victim, Lady Wheelhope), as seen in his frank admission of lies, or his willingness to disclose that he ignored his promises to McGill or George. The notion of a lie indeed is almost metaphor in this reading, since the local lies literally awaken the Archliar, who paradoxically gains Robert's soul with the most consummate lie of all, the lie which is never expressed in untruths—the Devil is scrupulously *honest*—but is a lie in its total context, in that the Devil mirrors Robert's hypocritical, lying but logical way of life with his own literally honest hypocrisy. Robert will become the Devil's man within a framework of apparently Christian language and action!

One cannot stress enough how traditional are the rules governing the scenes that follow. They are *not* Gothic, or fantastic in Hoffmann's manner (though many of the individual scenes, as opposed to the conditions governing them, seem to indicate that Hogg had indeed enjoyed his friend and Edinburgh fellow-novelist R. P. Gillies's translation of *Elixiere des Teufels*)[23] but belong to that tradition where the Devil has been identified as the Black Man since time out of mind, the world of "The Daemon Lover." Hogg sticks to Barnaby's ancient folk-rules faithfully. Barnaby had continued that "the bogles, they meddle wi' nane but the guilty; the murderer and the mansworn, and the cheater of the widow and fatherless, they do for them. . . ." Robert has eventually killed father, mother, brother and Blanchard; has lied about this; has cheated the widow Keeler of her land through corrupt lawyer Linkum (who is "quite well acquainted" with Gilmartin) and has ruined and murdered her fatherless daughter. Systematically he has qualified for "the bogles" to do for him—and, crimson pawed and nightmarish, they certainly do.

But this is to anticipate. As yet, Robert has only awakened the Devil's attentions, and it remains for the

Devil to manoeuvre Robert into a *free choice* of his own damnation. This is the main difference between the psychological and the supernatural interpretations. Where in the former he was the product of environment and conditioning, to be pitied, in the latter he is a free agent, and the Devil will scrupulously observe the rules of the "Game of Souls."

Hogg is extremely careful in this respect, and never more so than when handling that aspect of the relationship between Devil and Robert which I discussed under the blanket term of "possession" earlier. Robert is possessed in various ways at many times throughout the novel, but he is never, and must never be, possessed at the significant moment of moral choice, such as the moment of the shooting of Blanchard or the stabbing of George. The Devil is allowed to possess him as a result of sin, but not at the point where Robert chooses to perform the sin.

His first meeting with Satan is one in which he is partly possessed, the language describing the encounter conveying this. It is striking how the two figures draw together as though linked by a kind of spiritual umbilical cord, an "invisible power" that pulls "like the force of enchantment," their eyes meeting and mingling in a way that causes Robert acute bodily sensations. Robert describes how they stop, eyes fixed, a yard apart; yet the effect of the passage is to imply a much more profound merging of spirits in a curiously physical and claustrophobic sense. We *feel* Robert losing control over his own identity, as the stranger reads his thoughts and anticipates his very words. That is why Robert says he was "quite captivated," since he was, literally; and why he feels "deliverance" after. Even then he is not completely dis-possessed, his parents recognising that he is "transformed." Words have to be read literally in this novel. "I could not have known you for the same person," says his father, while Hogg with consummate irony has him further guess aright that "Satan, I fear, has been busy with you . . .", but discount this when he discovers that the stranger's ideas concurred with his own!

This ironic technique of Hogg's is ubiquitous and one of his outstanding successes in the novel. Truth presents itself in such a form that the burden of interpretation rests with the beholder, who makes as it were a moral choice in the selection of his version. For example, the Father of Lies at all points presents Robert with sufficient evidence to realise who he is. Not only is he sinister in appearance, but his Bible has the red characters traditionally used in folklore and Hogg's earlier tales from *The Mountain Bard* to his dramas and *The Three Perils of Man* to signify that the book is a manual of Evil. "I am indeed your brother . . . in my belief of the same truths, and my asurance in the same mode of redemption . . ." admits Satan to Robert, later confessing with superb use of Christian argument *against* itself that prayer is not for him since it is selfish, and that true humility demands that we accept our lot! He has one parent, whom he does not acknowledge, and he will not use his Christian name to Robert—the one he *does* use, by implication his non-Christian name, is the one best suited for Robert to use, he says.

> I am a being of a very peculiar temper, for though I have servants and subjects more than I can number, yet, to gratify a certain whim, I have left them . . . and . . . have attached myself only to you. . . .[23]

All this is quite true, and beautifully designed to keep

within the "rules" at the same time as causing Robert to exercise his pride in deciding that this must be Czar Peter who seeks *him* out! The Devil quotes scriptures with complete truth and authority, for as Penpunt later tells us, "Satan . . . was the firmest believer in a' the truths of Christianity that was out o' heaven . . . he had often been driven to the shift o' preaching it himsel. . . ." Gilmartin tells Robert

> My former days were those of grandeur and felicity. But, would you believe it? *I was not then a Christian.* Now I am. I have been converted to its truths by passing through the fire, and, since my final conversion, my misery has been extreme.[24]

There are none so blind as the Roberts who *will not* see, despite the fact that the rules also demand that agents of Good also warn Robert, in keeping with fair play. But ironically he *will* see them as Evil forces, and swallow the bait which allows the Devil to play him at the end of his line with wonderful sophistry. Can there be a more effective piece of irony in the novel than when Gilmartin employs Christian belief to bring about murder?

> If the man Blanchard is worthy, he is only changing his situation for a better one; and, if unworthy, it is better that one fall than that a thousand souls perish. Let us be up and doing. . . .[25]

This is irony of the most universal, finest kind. It cannot be argued of such examples that they take their effect *within* a Christian basis, for the pungency of the comment lies in its demonstration that the very texture of Christian belief is at times suspect, reflecting ideals which are incapable of realisation on earth, and also dangerously mis-construable. The nett effect of the

Devil's justified ability to cite Christian doctrine for his purposes is to exemplify the whole point of the novel; that it is not just a weakness in those like Lady Dalcastle in that she overstrains and deforms the tenets of the great reformers, but it is a profound weakness in the theology of the reformers themselves that allows the logical reasoning of the Bostons and Wringhims to derive conclusions so cruel and absurd from Christian premises. To that extent the novel *is* a satire on *formalised* religion, and the Devil's "honesty" is one of the most effective means Hogg uses to make this ironic comment.

In this light it is worth examining his name, Gil-martin, once more. Here again he is providing clues for Robert to use, since the name is associated with "Gil-moules" or "Gil-Mouly," a folk name for the Devil that Hogg himself uses at least on three occasions in poetry and drama, referring particularly to Gilmouly's ability to insinuate himself even through keyholes[26] and his ability to take whatever shape he wishes. And taken on the analogy of Gilpatrick, "servant or disciple of St Patrick," a possible popular reading of "Gilmartin" of the time could be "servant of the evil (or drunken) saint."[27] One recalls that Wringhim senior is just such a deep drinking "saint," as well as being the first justified sinner we meet in the book; the man whose prayers and curses employ the Devil; and last seen going off to Glasgow "with that strange mysterious person." Robert actually says that his friend is more attached to Wringhim senior than to anyone other than himself. The Reverend Wringhim has much to answer for, not the least being that he "fathered" the appearance of Gilmartin with his wrestling with "God" "in bitterness and anguish of Spirit" until he had prevailed against the serpent

170

turnings of that deity and gained that assurance that Robert was accepted by him.

It is significant that whenever Wringhim senior speaks at length a new intensity of evil results, and it is his appalling dedication of the boy to his Lord as a weapon to lay waste his enemies that extends the Devil's writ to include violence and murder. But as yet Robert has not committed himself this far; "though he often aroused my zeal to the highest pitch, still my heart at times shrunk from the shedding of life-blood." The Devil may have been given license to work on Robert by his and his father's previous wickedness, but Robert is far from suicide and damnation, which is the Devil's goal. The next event in Robert's decline is important, in that it enables us to deduce exactly what are the "rules" governing the Devil's right to control and possess Robert.

Robert knows not how to turn in the matter of Blanchard. He looks up to Heaven for guidance, and a dimness comes over his eyes, till through the cloudy veil which obscures Heaven come the points of golden weapons, directed towards him. Robert kneels, and *decides* to stretch out his hand to take one. This free decision must be set in context, for it establishes a vital "cycle" of free agency and demonic possession.

Before his decision, Robert has obviously been as doubtful of the good morality of what is being planned as at any time we meet him. *He himself* is genuinely pondering Good and Evil, and his instinct to seek Heavenly guidance is rewarded. This, note, angers Gilmartin, who frowns to see his victim looking for Heavenly advice; and worries him too, since Robert may freely decide to take this advice. The warning is given, the message being that Heavenly disapproval is represented by its golden weapons threatening

Robert, the offender. But Robert makes his moral choice, and in deciding that the vision furthers his intention to murder, enables Satan to rejoice that his moment of danger is past. As a result of Robert's evil decision, he is also permitted possession of Robert, and the usual symptoms of this present themselves in Robert's account. His mind is "exalted," he is "inflamed" in his zeal, and even more explicitly since Hogg means this to be taken literally,

> I was as one beside himself; which my parents perceived that night, and made some motions towards confining me in my room.[28]

He is himself *and* Satan, "greatly strengthened and encouraged that night." The cycle is established. Free thought results in a decision in principle, usually an evil intent. The Devil is then permitted possession, which takes Robert up to the next stage, the evil action itself. Here again he must be "delivered" back to himself and free action, as with the two murders we witness. He is then "helped off," till the cycle begins again, with remorse and free thought taking Robert towards the next, more evil, goal. In this cycle Heaven plays its part too, usually interposing an eleventh-hour warning like the "sweet voice" which whispers, "Beware," just before the Blanchard murder.

Using the "enchanting" little golden pistol that Gilmartin provides, Robert does the deed. Significantly, and as with the murder of George, it is solely his action. "Gilmartin's ball had not taken effect, which was altogether wonderful; as the old man's breast was within a few yards of him."

After skilfully leading Robert to the "easier" murder of one whose doctrines Robert hates, Gilmartin is ready to take Robert towards the even greater evil of fratricide. The remorse which he felt for Blanchard's death, and for the capture and trial of the journeyman preacher as a result, is cancelled by Robert's free decision to let the latter die. Consequently he feels "considerable zeal" for the notion of regular murder of opponents. But Gilmartin needs both more time to prepare Robert for this greater sin and more power. The first he achieves by letting Robert's mind chafe for a spell by withdrawing into the background temporarily, and later by having a "dress-rehearsal" on Arthur's Seat which, by having Robert come off badly, increases Robert's hate. The second he gains from that neglected but important curse of Wringhim and son following Robert's release from jail, whereby Wringhim

> gave up my father and brother, according to the flesh, to Satan, making it plain to all my senses of perception that they were being given up of God to be devoured by fiends of men . . . and that *whosoever* should slay them would do God good service.[29]

This is the same curse as in part one that set Satan on George's right hand. The Devil's skill from now on is consummate, as he praises Robert's "amiability" as "natural" (!), but gently argues that such are carnal weaknesses and bonds not as binding as "the Lord's." He also plays on a new motive, that of greed, by picturing to Robert the goodly uses to which *he* could put Dalcastle estate. Robert freely decides that he will kill his brother. Possession follows, and Robert's heart pants with eagerness to behold his brother, which is very different to his usual cowardice. He even says that "I found myself moved by the spirit within me," explicitly revealing his partial possession. Possession

173

takes him through the tennis matches, his friend telling him ironically that he does not know "one-half his might"—the other half, inside him, is Gilmartin.

One important new development in the pattern of possession does however occur following the curse and decision to kill George. Robert is seized with that strange distemper which is amnesia in the psychological interpretation, but *total* as opposed to partial possession in the supernatural reading. Frequent partial possession is now more frequently replaced by the total form. Why? The answer is that the Devil's ultimate aim of suicide, that final unpardonable sin, will not be brought about by partial possession as effectively as by doing terrible things either in Robert's likeness or through Robert's possessed body and then confronting Robert's shocked mind with the terrible impact of guilt. From this point on, too, the "love" relationship between the two slowly moves towards hate, since the Devil, sure of Robert being his man and lacking only the final signed pact and suicide, can be less devious and more direct in his manipulation. The decision of Robert to kill George and the curse which formally expressed it is in many ways the turning point in the "Game" for the Devil. One notices that just as the curse set Satan on George's right, it also created a mirror situation for Robert, whereby "another person" appeared to Robert in his "distemper"

always in the same position from the place where I sat or stood, which was about three paces of me towards my left.[30]

The Devil goads Robert by appearing to him as George, heightening his hate so that he runs "scarcely knowing what I did" to Arthur's Seat. As usual though the possession drops away immediately before the

174

murder attempt; Heaven sends the White Lady to keep the balance of Good and Evil—with the significant warning that Robert will forfeit his soul if he goes through with the attempt. As with the golden weapons vision, Gilmartin is enraged at the risk of losing control. Indeed remorse of a kind does foil this attempt, despite the Devil's fantastic diversion of George.

The actual murder is the last occasion that Gilmartin needs to stick to the "rules" of possession. Once Robert freely chooses to murder George the Devil simply helps Robert off in order to terrify him into suicide. It is even questionable whether Robert commits any of the crimes thereafter, since he has no memory of them and presumably has made no free choice to abandon sobriety and celibacy. Freedom of choice is no longer necessary, since his soul is forfeit. The Devil has him trapped, and only wishes to embarrass God further.

> Oh! It is a grand prize for him, an' a proud Deil is he, when he gangs hame to his ain ha', wi' a batch o' the souls o' sic strenuous professors on his back. . . .[31]

The Devil "frames" Robert into suicide, ruling out all possibility of repentance, by inducing despair and guilt, by even gloating and relishing Robert's distress, by parodying sympathy, resembling George, and even informing against Robert. Cleverly the Devil performs deeds which Robert feels he *might* have done, though he cannot remember, as when Robert admits that the idea of having a beautiful lady at his disposal has a certain attraction in it.

But the Devil does not need to maintain such subtlety. He now even lets Robert perceive his situation. "Either I had a second self who transacted business in my likeness, or else my body was at times possessed by a spirit over which it had no control." Robert's "secret" terrors that the Enemy has powers over him are encouraged by Gilmartin, as he appears to Robert virtually as a symbol of Hell.

> It bore the figure, air, and features of my late brother . . . yet in all these there were traits so forbidding, so mixed with an appearance of misery, chagrin, and despair, that I still shrunk . . . it was the voice of the great personage I had so long denominated my friend . . . and whose presence and counsels I now dreaded more than Hell. It was his voice. . . . They were the sounds of the pit, wheezed through a grated cranny. . . .[32]

The reader may feel at this point that Hogg is dragging out his tale too long, prolonging a struggle long since lost. But Heaven's mercy is infinite, and until Gilmartin has the pact and the suicide as a *fait accompli* he is not the total victor. All the previous warnings of earthly and Heavenly agents from Barnet and the Jailer to the voices and the White Lady are gathered together in a last, great Heavenly effort to get through to Robert in that series of parables told by Penpunt. The Auchtermuchty stories are the climax of the battle for Robert's soul. Here the details of demonic possession are spelled out unmistakeably to Robert, first directly, but unsuccessfully.

> I was so astounded at the terrible idea that had gone abroad regarding my fellowship with the Prince of Darkness, that I could make no answer. . . .[33]

A second effort is made by Penpunt, causing Robert to faint, but not to repent. The third is the magnificent, traditional Auchtermuchty tale, which expresses in microcosm and allegory the entire action of the novel. Auchtermuchty is fanatical Presbyterian Scotland, with even its wooing conducted in the language of the Song of Solomon. Here too in Auchtermuchty the Devil intends to catch sinners, "and with their own bait too," like Gilmartin with Robert. Just as the elders ignore Robin, so Robert ignored all his earthly and heavenly warnings. And there is a deeper, more disturbing level of allegory yet, in that the Auchtermuchty delight in damnation is perhaps parallelled in Robert himself. Robert has known, in his heart of hearts, like the Auchtermuchty people, that it is the Devil who assails him.

This last bitter irony raises a final nightmare speculation about Penpunt. He is, after all, a religious enthusiast himself, as a Cameronian. Could he be the Devil? Could the White Lady, as she promised, have been Heaven's last warning, and Penpunt's comments designed to drive Robert further into that misery necessary to push him to suicide? Certainly, when he tries Penpunt's "golden rule" on all his actions, to his despair—"Behold, not one of them could stand the test."

Hogg has been criticised for his last, mildly diabolic scenes. But they are the logical outcome to the supernatural story, as the Devil now reveals his full power, mocking Robert by pretending to save him. His becoming trapped in the weaver's web is surely a metaphor for his spiritual state, caught completely as he is in Gilmartin's snares, identified by the weaver as Satan himself, and cut off totally from communication with the world of ordinary humans that the weaver represents. There must be nowhere for Robert to go, no one to whom he can talk, and the terrors of

Hell's legions must be all around him. Thus is he driven to that final act which makes him Satan's prize for eternity.

* * *

The function of the third part is to bring the tension and fantastic atmosphere of the last part down to earth, so that the Editor can present the reader with a clear choice of interpretation. The Editor asks:

> What can this work be? Sure, you will say, it must be an allegory; or, as the writer calls it, a religious PARABLE, showing the dreadful danger of self-righteousness? I cannot tell. Attend to the sequel, which is a thing so extraordinary . . . that, if there were not hundreds of living witnesses to attest the truth of it, I would not bid any rational being believe it.[34]

I have already stressed how the end of the third part points us towards two mutually exclusive interpretations. Is this not emphasised by Hogg by the fact that he even *begins* the third part with the same Editorial ambiguity of response? Cleverly the part continues to balance the rational world against that of the older, traditional and supernatural world, with the cool scepticism of Edinburgh and John Gibson Lockhart as its representative, balanced against the inexplicable details of the death of Wringhim and the preservation of his corpse. The world of *Blackwood's Magazine* with all its modern, urban associations for the reader of Hogg's day, would enter the story like a breath of cool, familiar-tasting air after the ancient odours of the pit and the superstitious past. By using names of well-known figures like Lockhart and William Laidlaw, Hogg's Border farmer friend, as well as that

of Hogg himself, the reader would further reassure
himself that he was back in the land of the living. But
is there not a very real skill beyond even this? Does
the use of the familiar and modern not eventually
carry a real sting in its tail, as the reader realises that
even these household names are touched with wonder
and awe? There may be initial relief in the return to
objective pragmatism, but it ultimately serves only to
establish clearly the two poles of meaning between
which the story generates its charge of wonder.

It may be considered that in separating these two
poles I have dissipated much of the charge. This is
true, since the first enjoyment of this novel lies in the
very bewilderment of response, as the imagination and
reason battle to control the weird events. But in terms
of fully understanding both Hogg's great ingenuity,
with or without Lockhart's sharp wit to aid him, and in
terms of placing the novel at its crucial point in Hogg's
development, I feel that the dualistic complexity must
be unravelled to see how clearly Hogg wished to run
with both the hares and the hounds.

Has the novel a central issue towards which its
marvels and irony are directed? I think the answer to
this is in its use of the Lie as a motif which finally
becomes the central metaphor. The central "Lie" in the
novel is not a "logical" untruth, but an untruth which
lies at the heart of Christian theology, and allows the
whole fabric of "justified" egotism and social evil to
result. The novel highlights the intrinsic weakness of
Christian dogma in that it contains at its heart premises
which permit Robert to deduce the following:

The more I pondered on these things the more I saw
of the folly and inconsistency of ministers in spending
their lives striving and remonstrating with sinners in

179

order to induce them to do that which they had it not in their power to do. Seeing that God had from all eternity decided the fate of every individual that was to be born of woman, how vain was it in man to endeavour to save those whom their maker had, by an unchangeable decree, doomed to destruction. . . . How much more wise would it be, thought I, to begin and cut sinners off with the sword! [35]

This is the central issue of the novel. It is Christian and Presbyterian theology which allows Robert his justification for this. In *The Heart of Midlothian* the same system is found wanting by Jeannie Deans, who appeals to "nature's voice" to rescue her from the cruel trap she finds herself in between God's laws and man's laws. There is in both Hogg and Scott a profound desire to replace formal theology of this restricting and dangerous kind (in the sense that it can be taken to logical but frightening conclusions) with an instinctive and heart-centred humanitarian conscience. In Scotland it is a form of humanism which goes back to the eighteenth-century teachings in Glasgow University of Francis Hutcheson, and is found in works as diverse as Henry MacKenzie's *The Man of Feeling* (1771) and Burns's "Address to the Unco Guid" (1785). We have already seen that in *The Pilgrims of the Sun* Hogg showed a tendency to break with formalised Christianity, while his Wat of Chapel-hope in *The Brownie of Bodsbeck* trusted completely to heart and instinct in his dealings with *both* Episcopalians and Presbyterians. I am not suggesting that Hogg is implying in *The Justified Sinner* that Christianity is in its Presbyterian form evil and unwanted, but I do see this and much of his work, together with novels of Scott's like *Old Mortality* and

The Heart of Midlothian and John Galt's *Annals of the Parish* (1821) and *The Entail*, as expressions of a desire in nineteenth-century Scotland for a warmer, more humane, more secular and less doctrinaire response to private and public morality. It is significant that the warmest human beings of the book like the old Laird, his mistress, and Bell Calvert, are by Christian doctrine to be judged sinners. I do not think that Hoggs sees *them* as needing Christian forgiveness. Rather he asserts that they, like the prostitute Clifford who expressed the only real charity of *Basil Lee,* are representatives—symbols, perhaps—of a richer, deeper charity which wells up in the human heart from sources as mysterious to the Christian as to the agnostic.

Finally, it may be argued that the book's failure to resolve its dilemma of two conflicting interpretations involving two radically different attitudes to life represents its major failure. Far from thinking so, I would argue that in suspending his account of these moral actions between two bases of judgement Hogg has expressed a situation still of crucial importance and confusion for the present day. We are still torn now between ascribing guilt to the social offender, adjudging him evil, and deducing on the other hand the circumstances of heredity, background and environment which determined the anti-social action. Hogg has merely presented us with the extrapolated polarities of each way of thinking, in a story which still never fails to create unease and wonder—because it echoes the polarised bases of our own moral judgements.

NOTES

1. Although the date of publication of *An Edinburgh Bailie* is 1835, it appears from his letters to Blackwood that it was written about the same time as *The Justified Sinner*. This is discussed in the next chapter.

2. *Fraser's Magazine*, vol. II, 1830, p. 530.

3. *The Justified Sinner* (hereinafter *Sinner*), 1947 ed., p. 165.

4. Lockhart and Hogg were certainly up to something funny in the way of literary collaboration at this time. I have discovered in the unpublished second volume of A. L. Strout's *The Life and Letters of James Hogg* (in the National Library of Scotland) the copy of a most peculiar letter to Lockhart of October 4, 1832. In this Hogg makes the strange suggestion that Lockhart should write "Sir Walter's life [Scott having just died] in my [Hogg's!] name and in my manner," so that he will enjoy greater freedom than he would otherwise have as Scott's son-in-law. "It will likewise do me some credit as a biographer . . . Think of this my dear Lockhart and *depend upon it it shall be an Adam Blair* no living shall ever know of it and if you think it necessary I shall copy it all with my own hand or get the sheets copied here as you write them and let them all be transmitted from this to the publisher." (Strout, vol. II, p. 72).

   This obviously hints at some previous and secret collaboration—ostensibly *Adam Blair,* Lockhart's novel about a lunatic published in 1822. As Simpson asked (without knowing of this letter, but disliking the idea of Saintsbury and others that Hogg didn't write *The Justified Sinner*), "Did Hogg also write *Adam Blair*?" (*Simpson,* p. 193). The evidence of the letter is tantalisingly cryptic, a shorthand between the friends who had already "collaborated" on the *Chaldee Manuscript.* Is Hogg suggesting a *quid pro quo*? *Adam Blair* is hardly Hogg's style, but it is not impossible that in these years of closeness to Lockhart he perhaps helped the young writer with ideas and advice. What then more likely than that Lockhart would discuss Hogg's novel of similar theme with Hogg? That he should assist with ideas of structure, and possibly with the control of the difficult passages of theological debate between Gilmartin and Robert?

This would add point to the use of Lockhart, in typical Chaldee fashion in the last part—adding humour to the fact that Lockhart deprecates Hogg's "ingenious lies." There may be more than chance in the fact that in this part Lockhart, "as he had so many things of literature and law to attend to that he would never think more of it," presents the Sinner's account to the Editor, who then makes it into the novel. The entire matter of degree of authorial responsibility in both *Adam Blair* and *Justified Sinner* must remain an unsolved and fascinating riddle.

5. *Simpson,* pp. 170-173.

6. *Simpson,* pp. 190-192.

7. G. H. Millar, *A Literary History of Scotland,* 1902, pp. 302-303.

8. B. R. Bloedé, "James Hogg's *Private Memoirs and Confessions of a Justified Sinner*; the genesis of the double," *Etudes Anglaises,* vol. 26, no. 2, p. 186.
   Ian Campbell, "Author and Audience in Hogg's *Confessions*," *Scottish Literary News,* vol. 2, no. 4, 1972, pp. 66-76.

9. *Sinner,* pp. 229-230.

10. There is an excellent analysis of the pattern of division and its significance in the novel in David Eggenschwiler's "James Hogg's *Confessions* and the Fall into Division" in *Studies in Scottish Literature,* vol. 9, 1971-72, pp. 26-39.

11' L. L. Lee, "The Devil's Figure; James Hogg's Justified Sinner," *Studies in Scottish Literature,* vol. 3, 1966, pp. 230-239.

12. *Sinner,* p. 77.

13. *Sinner,* p. 31.

14. *Sinner,* p. 28.

15. *Sinner,* p. 72.

16. *Sinner,* p. 91.

17. *Sinner,* p. 99.

18. *Sinner,* pp. 105-6.

19. *Sinner,* p. 138.

20. *Sinner,* p. 140.

21. *Tales,* vol. I, p. 99.

22. Hogg would have to have had a "preview" of this, since it also came out in 1824.

23. *Sinner,* p. 118.

24. *Sinner,* p. 174.

15. *Sinner*, p. 122.

26. "Gilmoules" and "Gilmouly" are used in an invocation to the Devil in the play *All-Hallow-Eve*. The witch chants "Where is Gil Moules/Where is Gil Moules/Works he not save when the Tempest howls?" *Dramatic Tales*, 1817, p. 56. He is "Gil-Moules" in the poem "Superstition and Grace" and the poem "A Witch's Chant." *Works*, vol. II, pp. 375 and 396 respectively.

27. "Gilpatrick" from *Surnames of the United Kingdom*, Henry Harrison, 1912, vol. I, p. 164.
"Martin" as "drunken saint" from *An Etymological Dictionary of the Scottish Language*, 1880, vol. 3, p. 239. I am indebted to Mrs R. N. W. Smith of St Andrews for these suggestions.

28. *Sinner*, p. 126.

29. *Sinner*, p. 137.

30. *Sinner*, p. 139.

31. *Sinner*, p. 179.

32. *Sinner*, pp. 170-171.

33. *Sinner*, p. 177.

34. *Sinner*, p. 217.

35. *Sinner*, p. 112.

In addition to comments on the novel by critics like Edith Batho, and others cited in Simpson, the following modern material is valuable:

Ian Campbell, "Hogg's *Confessions of a Justified Sinner*," *Liturgical Review*, vol. 2, 1972, pp. 28-33.

John Carey, *Introduction* to his edition of *The Justified Sinner*, 1969.

David Craig, *Scottish Literature and the Scottish People*, pp. 195-96.

R. Kiely, *"The Private Memoirs and Confessions of a Justified Sinner,"* in *The Romantic Novel in England*, 1973, pp. 208-232.

Coleman Parsons, *Witchcraft and Demonology in Scott's Fiction*, 1964, pp. 287-297.

Douglas Mack, "Hogg's Religion and *The Confessions of a Justified Sinner*," *Studies in Scottish Literature*, vol. 7 no. 4, 1970, pp. 272-5.

Kurt Wittig, *The Scottish Tradition in Literature*, pp. 247-250.

I have not included material mentioned already in the notes in this list.

CHAPTER SIX

FICTION AND POETRY
1825-35

FOR ALL the thematic brilliance, shockingly effective presentation, and ingenious ambiguity of *The Justified Sinner,* it was one of Hogg's biggest flops. Only two magazines bothered to review it at all, and those in terms that were dauntingly familiar to Hogg. *The Westminster Review* regretted that

> the author did not employ himself better than in uselessly and disgustingly abusing his imagination, to invent wicked tricks for a mongrel devil, and blasphemous lucubrations for an insane fanatic.[1]

The New Monthly thought that

> Nothing more completely ridiculous can well be imagined than the whole of the story. . . . We do not altogether approve of the mode which the author has chosen of attacking the religious prejudices of numbers, who, notwithstanding their speculative opinions, are in no danger of becoming either parricides or fratricides . . . these Confessions . . . are singularly dull and revolting . . . and it is altogether unfair to treat the reader with two versions of such extraordinary trash as the writer has given us . . . we do most solemnly protest against the iniquity of bad English. . . .[2]

These opinions must powerfully have endorsed the views of all at *Blackwood's* that Hogg was not a novelist. From now on that magazine's policy towards his ambitious, novel length fiction was to ignore it either when it was offered to them or when it was published elsewhere.

It would, however, be by no means true to say that Hogg was totally demoralised from this point on. It was a turning point, but its significance was not immediately obvious in Hogg's work. He was even now working on a novel and some novelettes, all of which were further efforts to vary the approaches he had already tried and failed with, and all of which were nevertheless descendants of *Basil Lee, The Three Perils of Man,* and *The Justified Sinner.* In this conjecture I have been aided immensely by Alan Strout's unpublished typescript of the second volume of his *The Life and Letters of James Hogg,* which is in the National Library of Scotland.[3] From evidence of Hogg's letters (as well as from his *Autobiography*) it seems virtually certain that *Some Remarkable Passages in the Life of An Edinburgh Bailie,* a novel told in the first person with a hero as inglorious and petty-minded as either Basil Lee or Robert Wringhim, "The Adventures of Colonel Peter Aston," "A Few Remarkable Adventures of Sir Simon Brodie," "Some Passages in the Life of Colonel Cloud" and "The Baron St. Gio" were all written at the same time as *The Justified Sinner.* Together these tales were to make up two volumes to be called *Lives of Eminent Men.* To this we must add the fact that two more novelettes, "The Surpassing Adventures of Allan Gordon" and "The Adventures of Captain John Lochy" were at the very least well under way in 1827 and 1829 respectively.[4]

This evidence drastically re-arranges our awareness of Hogg's last ten years. It means that all his ambitious work in fiction can be dated to the period of *The Justified Sinner.* The fact that it did not appear till several years later—and in the case of *An Edin-*

burgh Bailie over a decade later—shows on one hand that Hogg was finding extreme difficulty in finding any one to publish his novels and long tales, and on the other that, although the last few years of his life *appear* eventful in terms of fiction, they were in fact years of disillusionment, obsession about his publishing problems, and eventual "drying up."

Here we must be on our guard against Hogg's own opinion of his work, always unreliable. Unfortunately Louis Simpson—to his great credit the only critic so far to consider the range of Hogg's fiction—fell into this trap when he argued that "we may pass over his unimportant writings, most of which Hogg himself excluded in planning a collected edition."[5] Hogg was increasingly in these last ten years to demean his own novels. He disparaged *The Three Perils of Man,* cutting out all the superb folk-lore and diablerie for the 1837 collection; he savaged *The Justified Sinner,* removing the Auchtermuchty stories and shortening the religious debates; and did not include many excellent later stories of the supernatural or the fantastic. Significantly, nearly all these stories were published in *The Edinburgh Literary Journal* or *Fraser's Magazine*[6] after having been turned down by *Blackwood's*, which reinforces the idea that Hogg did not trust his own judgement in these later years, but accepted that what Blackwood published was by definition his best work. In the 1832 version of his *Autobiography* he is at sixty-two not the same self-confident man who had bluntly told off those who criticised his *Winter Evening Tales*.

Woe be to that reader who goes over a simple and interesting tale fishing for indelicacies, without calculating on what is natural for the characters . . .

a practice too common among the people of the present age, especially if the author be not a bluestocking. . . .[7]

By 1832, as Hogg looks over what now seems to the modern critic to be his period of greatest achievement, that which produced his finest novels, he refers to the details of these novels as "circumstances of importance to nobody but myself." He apologises for the "medley" he made of *The Three Perils of Man,* ruining "what might have been made one of the best historical tales our country ever produced" with "such a mass of diablerie as retarded the main story and rendered the whole perfectly ludicrous." At the time of writing he had thought it in a better style than his best. "I was all this time writing as if in desperation, and see matters now in a different light," says the older Hogg, telling us further that since *The Justified Sinner* was "a story replete with horrors," "it was published anonymously, and of course did not sell very well . . . for I do not remember ever receiving anything for it. . . ."[8]

The failure of *Lives of Eminent Men* was the final blow to Hogg's major ambitions in fiction. By considering *Eminent Men* here, with the related, slightly later novelettes, "John Lochy" and "Allan Gordon," we can round off that decade within which Hogg tried and failed to be a successful novelist.

An Edinburgh Bailie is the third of that group of novels of which *Basil Lee* and *The Justified Sinner* are the others. All are told principally by mean, selfish protagonists who obviously are creations of, and not spokesmen for, Hogg, which separates them in kind from say, Wat of Chapelhope in *The Brownie of Bodsbeck* or Charlie Scott of *The Three Perils of Man,* where these heroes stand for values which Hogg shares fully. All draw their power from their being, as Bloedé said of *The Justified Sinner*, "an exteriorization of Hogg's own conflicts,"[9] in that all present a vulnerable, naive fellow who is vain, ambitious, but out of his depth. In all the arch-enemy or enemies, who seem inextricably linked in bonds of hate that involve a curious attraction, decide their fate. In all there is a curious frankness of that kind we meet in Defoe or Boswell, whereby the reader is convinced with a strangely compelling yet distasteful honesty. In all, but especially in the last two, demonic metaphors are used to designate the hated enemy and to suggest an alternative interpretation of events.

The Bailie is Archibald Sydeserf, "bred in the strictest principles of the Reformation," who describes his adventures to us in a language close to that of Wringhim—"my heart was lifted up; but alas! soon was it sunk down again in gall and bitterness." With a strange mixture of tones ranging from the "holier-than-thou" to the ashamed, he tells us of his shifting fortunes during the period of the sixteen-forties in Scotland, when Montrose fought for King and Episcopacy against the men of the Covenant and their principal leader, Argyle. Sydeserf changes sides rather easily, and, like Galt's Provost, always with a canny eye to the main chance. From starting as a humble secretary in Edinburgh Castle he becomes Argyle's right-hand man, as well as being an honoured Edinburgh Bailie. But the stepping stones of his political career have little interest for us. Hogg is so little a historical novelist that he employs the old device of an Editor to "present" the account to us, and noticeably the Editor steps in whenever the narrative demands some political or historical perspective.

189

We must now pass over several years, the history of which is entirely made up of plot and counterplot, raising and disbanding of armies, projects of great import, all destroyed by the merest accident,— truculent treaties, much parade and small execution; and follow our redoubted Bailie once more to the field of honour, the place of all others for which he was least fitted, and on which he valued himself most.[10]

Hogg has no ability or feeling at all for history as a force such as Scott analyses in *Old Mortality* or Galt in *Ringan Gilhaize*. But it is equally obvious in all his work that it is only where history outcrops into the vividly remembered folk tradition, or acts as background to his interest in the psychologically warped central figure, that Hogg goes through these unconvincing, formally necessary manoeuvres. That is not to say that he cannot describe battles, or re-tell folk history with authority; some of the battle scenes in this novel rank with the best of *The Three Perils of Man* and his less ambitious but straightforward and powerful acounts of Border skirmishes.

One feature of this novel, completely separate from its being in the slightest sense a "historical" novel, gives it a vitality that keeps it alive and worth saving now, apart from its interest as being bedfellow to *The Justified Sinner*. It is the atmosphere that Hogg manages to create whenever he touches on the strange, fated relationship between George Gordon, Lord of Enzie, and Sydeserf, and the broader echoes of that central relationship, which holds the entire book together in a kind of unity which crumbles at the edges whenever the plot moves temporarily away from it.

Sydeserf is visited in Edinburgh Castle by the beautiful Lady Jane Gordon, who manages to persuade him to turn traitor to his post and beliefs by giving her the evidence against her father, the Marquess of Huntly, a prisoner in the castle for treason. It is at this point that Hogg begins that strange description of Sydeserf's relations with the Huntly family which is so comparable to the way in which he described the relations of Gilmartin to Robert Wringhim. Here is the very language of Wringhim's enchantment, as Sydeserf deals with one whom it is suggested may be of that unearthly band of beautiful enchantresses of *The Hunt of Eildon* and the later "Mary Burnet"—a feeling developed when we discover that, like the sisters of *The Hunt of Eildon* there are twin Gordon sisters who are uncannily alike in their looks and witching manners. "Heaven knows" how the family steals his loyalty; talking of his movements with Jane round the castle, Sydeserf tells an accosting guard, "The Devil he has a right to move freely"—and there is no doubt Hogg means this to carry the literal inference as so often before. He is even given Huntly family livery of green and gold, which is always in Hogg a sign of unearthly presences.

What else but enchantment to account for such a Wringhim-like figure giving up career and covenant in his utter devotion to the Catholic family? And at the heart of this family is Enzie, "a perfect demon in pride and irritability," who immediately hates Sydeserf, and takes his hate out on him in one of these disgusting, embarrassing, but undoubtedly powerful scenes where the cowardice and pettiness of Sydeserf comes into the open as Enzie beats him before his beloved Jane. Hogg conveys the whining sense of degradation, the shame, and the hatred with total conviction. There is in addition that implication of madness which he evokes so well. The shame is intolerable, so Sydeserf comes to terms with it in a way we recognise.

> From that day forth I was impressed with a notion that Providence would not suffer any man to escape with impunity who had wronged me, and inherited my curse and malison.[11]

This is the Christian Sydeserf's comment as he watches a former tyrannical castle Governor hang for his, Sydeserf's murder! Cleverly Hogg makes the nasty Sydeserf stand complacently watching, and, moreover, find a Christian comfort and message for himself in terms of his hate for Enzie, while again and again the wretch protests innocence. This is a consistent and deliberate creation on Hogg's part, for we find the covenanting Sydeserf who weeps when his Jane prays to the virgin performing with exactly the same double standard when in battle. He takes no part in the dangerous siege of Aberdeen—but when it comes to the question of plundering after surrender, there is much of Galt's *Provost* in his thinking.

> I confess I voted for it, thinking my brave towns-men would have enjoyed it so much. I know it was reported to my prejudice, that I expected a principal share of the plunder myself . . . whoever raised that report, had no further ground for it than that I voted for the majority, several of them servants and ministers of the Lord.[12]

And like Wringhim, when his arch-enemy Huntly is humbled and taken prisoner to Edinburgh, he tells us

> It was marrow to my bones to see him thus . . . I

thought of his felling me down, and kicking me in the mud, when I was in a situation in which I durst not resist.[13]

But which of these enemies is morally worst is a moot point, as the Editor suggests, since by the climax of the novel all have come to realise that the Bailie has indeed some "indefinable power" over Enzie, which ends in Enzie's execution in Edinburgh as a direct result of the Bailie's hate. The moral ambiguity is finally stressed in the last sentence of the novel, referring to the Bailie's own death, following the execution of his leader, Argyle.

His body was carried to Elgin, the original burial place of his fathers, and by a singular casualty, his head laid precisely at the Marquess of Huntly's [Enzie's] feet.[14]

Herein lies the book's greatest weakness, seen before in that curious Border amorality of *The Three Perils of Man,* and possibly kept at bay in *The Justified Sinner* by the advising hand of Lockhart. In the end the ambiguity here relates to no such human debate as that of the rational against the supernatural, but merely *expresses* Hogg's powerful neurosis about a conspiracy by people in high places (including "friends" with whom he must continue to associate on apparently friendly terms, like Scott, Wilson, Blackwood and Lockhart) against his naive but justified aspirations to equality with them in matters creative and social. Consequently the figure of the Bailie is not linked to a recognisable consistent moral structure. He is in fact not always petty or mean—but devotedly serves the old Marquis of Huntly in a spirit of near-charity; can be generous to his defeated opponents, like the old warrior Gordon of Glenbucket, whom he treats with outstanding humanity when Gordon is his prisoner; and attends the Duke of Argyle, his final master, to the scaffold, with admirable loyalty.

It is quite clear here that while Hogg has the old command of local incident and dramatic event, with his astonishing ability to evoke the convincing tactual or emotional detail, he has lost all overall direction. The reason for this becomes obvious as one looks at the associated tales of *Eminent Men*. After the pronouncements of Scott on his use of diablerie he had "hidden" this element in *The Justified Sinner*. That stratagem too had failed, so, apart from the remnants of devil metaphor and fairy imagery which eventually lead to nothing, there is no other level of the traditional supernatural in these tales. A real and vital source of creativity for Hogg has for the moment closed itself off. The tragedy of this can only be estimated, since the tales still possess compelling moments. One of Hogg's most disturbing short stories is "The Baron St. Gio" in this series, with its strange *Caleb Williams* relationship between Kendale and the sinister murderer Mr Southman with echoes still of the unearthly powers of Gilmartin in the metaphors used ("It was the cloven foot of Satan") and his very name. Description of shocking murder was always Hogg's *forte,* and never better than here. Southman is one of his most convincing figures of evil, *implying* his power rather than revealing it—though when he does act it is horrible enough. Love and hate bind Kendale and Southman in strange bonds—

The man was very kind to me all the way, and good to the horses; but yet I could not endure to look at him. He had a still, round whitish face, and eyes as if he had been half sleeping, but when they glimmered up, they were horribly disagreeable.[15]

Yet, having witnessed the murders, Kendale becomes Southman's steward, through Southman's "persuasion." Here again is Hogg's preoccupation with unnatural fellowship, with yet again the teller of the tale revealing his own cowardice, through that curious frankness which so holds our attention. Here again is that *Brownie of Bodsbeck* sense of impenetrable mystery, with the autobiographer bewildered, but telling us enough to see more than he does.

But as with *An Edinburgh Bailie* there is no moral relevance to the tale, since out of all this evil Kendale acquires his title and fortune. To mix unwillingly in evil seems to lead to prosperity in these tales, and nowhere more so than in a novelette which is not in *Eminent Men,* but is clearly close to them in time and insists on consideration with them. "John Lochy," written slightly later, shows how the loss of the supernatural framework of tradition not only cost Hogg a layer of significance, but also a moral basis of a crude kind, in default of which his tales become pointless. Lochy is highborn, but mysteriously shut out from his rightful place; horrifically persecuted in youth, lonely, always aware of "a power combined against my life which I could not elude." Here too is the anti-romantic attitude to war of *Basil Lee,* but watered down, as Lochy pursues the path of a rather ignoble soldier of fortune: " 'Colonel, what shall we do?' said I. 'Hem! Hem!' said he. So we turned and retreated with the rest." But persecution by great ones continues all his life, against which he has only the "friendship" of the mysterious Fin, who is by day a peasant, by night the Baron Steinberg, a creature "devoid of any principle" who is generally believed to be the Devil. But as with his other recent tales of this kind, Hogg is half-hearted in his diabolic hints, as indeed in the entire fabric of this tale, which is a mish-mash of leavings from the more confidently told earlier versions. There is a failure of creative nerve here, so that where earlier he had defiantly asserted the unconventional behaviour of the prostitute Clifford as valid, thereby also asserting his own creative identity, Hogg retreats now into half-suggestions of Lochy being the illegitimate son of the Duke of Argyle, or half-suggestions of Fin being the Devil, with a milk-and-water picaresque element running throughout. Even so, the story has its force—but significantly the clearest memory one retains is of *loneliness*. Seeing others' good fortune, Lochy

> rejoiced . . . but I felt a blank in my heart, and as if I had been a creature deserted,—an isolated and lonely being, who seemed thrown upon the world to be a football in it; a creature,—the sport of every misadventure that could fall to the lot of man. . . .[16]

This certainly echoes Hogg's own frequent and plaintive letters to Blackwood from 1820 onwards. He grew more and more confused and angry about the misrepresentations and distortions of himself in the "Noctes," lost more and more money on Mount Benger, and got into deeper and deeper financial trouble, yet was unable to gauge the mode of fiction that would succeed, or find publishers for what he did write. Like Lochy, he too saw himself as the sport of fortune, "a tennis ball between contending parties," as he complained to Blackwood.

"Peter Aston," a novelette in *Eminent Men,* deserves

little attention, being in the Gothic mould of Hogg's poem "Young Kennedy," and only notable for the fact that even here there is an intense relationship of hatred which binds young Aston to his sweetheart's ferocious father. But two of the other tales in *Eminent Men* are very significant in Hogg's later development, in that they begin the last new and creatively valid stage that was to take place in Hogg's career.

Hogg had been told that the world of diablerie, peopled with devils and brownies and wizards and all sorts of grotesque creatures, was no longer permissible in polite letters. Given that this was the world in which his fantastic imagination gained its full freedom to wander, producing "The Witch of Fife," *The Three Perils of Man* and *The Justified Sinner* as the poetic and prose high points of what was his most important genre, he was now in trouble, in that this area of rich release was closed to him. We have seen how this immediately affected the quality of his fiction, and it is evidence of the real resilience and fecundity of his imagination that almost immediately he turned into a new avenue of non-supernatural comic release in "Colonel Cloud" and "Simon Brodie," continuing after to explore this in the novelette "Allan Gordon" and other "tall tales" like "The Marvellous Doctor," "The Pongos," "The Strange Letter of a Lunatic" and "The Separate Existence of Soul." Most of these stories have never been considered by modern critics, for Blackwood refused to publish most of them, and Hogg gave them to magazines which he considered less important. Consequently along with some other very fine ghost stories also published in these "lesser" magazines, Hogg did not bother to include these when he planned his collected works.

"Colonel Cloud" is a "mysterious gentleman" who

lives two rôles in life. As Hogg meets him at first, he is a courteous, urbane soldier-about-town, who comes in Hogg's way with strange frequency. (He even shares Hogg's own real-life deep-drinking experiences of his early period in Edinburgh when, before he got back to Altrive in 1815, he got into wild company in the Right and Wrong Club, with its deliberate reversal of conventional morality.)[17] There is a real topsy-turvy humour to the tale, with Hogg gradually realising that the Colonel is the nicest kind of complete impostor, revealed when they fish together by the Colonel's self-important misuse of rod and river, and exaggeration of minnow to whale. Hogg's own charity emerges in the story with his good-natured laughter at being taken in. Hearing that the deputy Adjutant-general to the Emperor of Austria is in reality a common weaver in a village near Alloa, Hogg sees "the Colonel's" claims as they are.

> I thought of the Castle of Coalpepper—the great staff officer—the square rigged brigandine—the Empress —the Colonel's carriage with three outriders—the dogs—the rural sports—and a thousand other things beside, all vanished in a breath.[18]

Does it not tell us much of Hogg to hear his characteristic response to having been so lied to, on such a scale, when he hears that for all these peculiarities, "the Colonel" is "sober, industrious, and a most kind and affectionate son"?

> "That is enough for me," said I in my heart; "Jacob and the shepherd shall be friends still. . . ."[19]

More ambitious than this, but in the same exuberant

and deliberately ridiculous and inflated idiom, is the novelette "Simon Brodie." There are comic scenes of far-fetched and fantastic caricature here that are superb, as when the seal rescues Sir Simon from drowning by falling in love with him and amorously edging him shore-wards. Sir Simon himself is obviously part Don Quixote and part Baron Bradwardine, and while overdone, nevertheless attains a real comic stature at moments, with his fearless stupidity and epic misadventures, his rusty sword and huge stiff cart horse. It is a great pity that Hogg began this story with the irrelevant *Bridal of Polmood* flirtations of the great Montrose and his friends at Sir Simon's Castle. The tale is really nothing to do with the Wars of Montrose or these incongruous and boring love adventures in Hogg's worst mixture of deceitful minxes and high-flown manners.

Far more successful is a slightly later novelette, "Allan Gordon." Here Hogg gives free reign to his fantasies, and produces a comic saga of a Scottish sailor who is wrecked and marooned at the North Pole. Of course the tale is utterly ridiculous, but it demonstrates the rather limited humour of the day that any critic should have expected anything else from what is so obviously the tallest of tall tales, a fantastic journey and adventure not meant to be taken any more seriously than "The Witch of Fife." And like that poem, there is paradoxically real beauty to be found in Hogg's descriptions of the clear-skyed North of his imagination, and Allan's cave four hundred feet up an iceberg, "like a chrystal dome, perfectly brilliant . . . when the sun shone, it had all the colours of the rainbow." Like Allan, we can imagine that there is something sublime in his iceberg home rolling through the polar seas, with a sky as pure as ether, and the lower shelves of his iceberg spreading into the deeps of the sea.

> There I was, reposing at my ease, or walking in awful sublimity on top of a lofty mountain, moving on with irresistible power and splendour. Without star or compass, without sail or rudder, there I was journeying on in the light of a sun that set not, solely in the Almighty's hand, to lead and direct me whither-so-ever he pleased. The fowls of heaven occasionally roosted in thousands on my mountain, and regarded me only as a fellow creature. . . .[20]

No one can surpass Hogg's fantastic imagination when it comes into full stride. With astonishing clarity of imagery the shepherd describes the Aurora Borealis, or the awful spectacle of the iceberg ripping up sheets of ice, "rolled up like a scroll before the mountain." How strange it is that this lyrical background so succeeds as the setting for Allan Gordon's love affair with a polar bear called Nancy, a relationship that both works for them and, in terms of humorous effect, for the reader. One feels real sorrow in parting, after many adventures, with Nancy, who has killed a dangerous bear who wanted her and attacked Allan. Who else but Hogg could reach out into the psychology of the female polar bear, and take our interest—albeit comically—with him? After the bloody battle,

> Though she licked my hand and my wound, and was as kind and gentle as ever, I could not help observing, with pain and a share of terror, that there was a gloomy gleam in her eye which I had never witnessed before. Her look was quite altered. It

was heavy, sullen, and drowsy; but when she looked up there was something of madness in it.

It is a delightful send-up of *Robinson Crusoe,* and having been successful here, Hogg tried twice more in "The Pongos" and "A Letter from Canada" to continue the formula. As always, when Hogg tries repeatedly to recapture a good thing, he fails. "The Pongos," with its ourang-outangs raising children in Africa in what must be the earliest version of the *Tarzan* story, lacks both the humour and the fabulous setting to sustain it; and while "A Letter from Canada" anticipates some of Robert Service's tallest stories like "The Cremation of Sam McGee" in its account of whole tribes being melted from their ice-coffin back into life, it is a late tale (1833) with none of the zest and colour of "Allan Gordon."

Hogg was to continue this vein for a few years more, with stories like "George Dobson's Expedition to Hell," "The Marvellous Doctor," "Dr David Dale's Account of a Grand Aerial Voyage," "The Strange Letter of a Lunatic," "An Awfu' Leein'-like Story" and "On the Separate Existence of the Soul." These, like his poems in the tradition of comic extravaganza, are some of his funniest and liveliest tales. Space precludes analysis of each, but in their pace, riotous imagination, and sheer good humour they contain some of Hogg's finest writing. They are not ironic, or complex in any way, but straightforward pieces of release for Hogg's vivid powers of fantasy. In them we respectively travel to Hell with a reluctant coachman; witness the riotous adventures of a grotesque botanist who has discovered a love-elixir which has "turned the world upside-down and inverted the whole order of nature," causing the first ladies of Spain (and love-maddened Bulls too, unfortunately) to pursue him

201

in droves in an inversion of the "May of the Moril Glen" situation; sail off in a balloon to the moon with the Ettrick Shepherd declaiming the moon's beauty in some spirited verse and quaffing vast amounts of Glenlivet; see a strange old man on Castle Hill offer snuff to a poor innocent who is then plagued by being two versions of the same person; dig up graves at night to find far from dead hard-drinking lairds; and finally discover Hogg, obsessed as always with doubles, swopping the body of Robin the old-fashioned shepherd with his laird, the new-fangled young agriculturalist, with ludicrous results, as they try to reconcile their strange new bodies with their old ideas. These fresh, unpretentious stories, dominated by the Spirit of Misrule and breathless in their comedy, have sadly been out of print since they first appeared.

In this last period Hogg brought out his tales as and when he could, with the result that many were published well after their time of writing. Hogg also had an opportunistic habit of loosely assembling tales around a rather arbitrarily chosen running title. Thus *The Shepherd's Calendar* of 1829 collects together tales which are only part of a country theme by the hair of their heads—like "The Marvellous Doctor" or "George Dobson" already categorised as fantastic tales of release. Similarly the *Tales of the Wars of Montrose* of 1835 pressed comic riots like "Sir Simon Brodie" into service as historical pieces illustrating the general theme, whereas most of the tales therein had been written for another collection entirely (*Eminent Men*), and, one suspects, quickly "became" Montrose Tales by dint of a sentence or two stuck at the front simply saying that the following happened in the time of the wars of the Covenant. For this reason I have preferred to ignore what seem to be the important collections of

1829, 1832, 1835, going instead to the evidence for the order of writing of the tales, and deducing a very different picture than that which the collection dates suggest.

This approach works especially with the tales we have already discussed, revealing that Hogg only reluctantly gave up the notion of writing novels, and showing his resourceful development of new approaches. But since he was only to write tales seriously for a few years more, with little or nothing of originality coming from his pen after 1831, we may now fairly take the rest of his tales as a whole and swiftly separate the real achievement from the increasingly pointless "balaam" (as he himself would have described much of it).[22]

Without doubt the real achievement of the last years of story-writing lies in the dozen or so excellent short stories of the supernatural, written for the most part between 1827 and 1830. While allowing that Hogg's stories of simple release are major achievements in their own way, they could not hope to compete with the kind of fiction Hogg wrote when drawing on his "Mountain and Fairy" background. Of course there is nothing to rival *The Three Perils of Man* or *The Justified Sinner* in these last tales. Hogg was demoralised by their reception to the point where he never again attempted anything sustained in this kind. But in a curious, intuitive, and ultimately quite cunning way he must both have known that this was of all subject-matters peculiarly his own, and that by presenting these tales as strange relics of a quaint Border past he could evade criticisms of vulgarity, and have them accepted by Blackwood and polite Edinburgh as the legitimate produce of their Ettrick Shepherd. They came in short doses, after all, and perhaps Hogg gauged that in this fashion he could still make his diablerie palatable.

Leaving aside the non-fiction accounts of the shepherd's life, describing matters like storms, dogs, sheep, the people the shepherd would meet, and the like, which are deliberately written against the Wilsonian and kailyard view of such matter, and are consequently superbly unsentimental and graphic accounts of the realities of a way of life rapidly vanishing, there are a handful of stories here which deserve to be in any representative collection of the best Scottish writing in the short story. When choosing a representative example of Hogg for a collection of Scottish nineteenth-century stories in 1970, I found that unlike Scott, or Galt, or even Stevenson, I was not presented with a fairly simple choice from two or three stories, but rather from a round dozen. Eventually I reduced these to this handful of superb examples of traditional tales of the Scottish Borders re-presented by Hogg, without nineteenth-century additions, and without losing the archetypal depth of their ancient folk themes and situations. Here Hogg is closest to the Ballads. Once more, Hogg's tale is traditional, and once more he unerringly sees his way.

These tales range from the "essential" supernatural situation for Hogg of a dream, wraith, or apparition which starkly foretells death and tragedy, to the full use once again of the whole colourful range of other world visitors from the brownie and the Devil to the witch and the wee, wee man; with the full use of traditional spells and metamorphoses. The finest of the "simpler" group, which includes "The Laird of Cassway," "The Fords of Callum," "The Unearthly Witness," "A Strange Secret," "A Tale of the Martyrs" and "Adam Scott" (to name only the more

204

successful tales of dream and apparition) are "The Barber of Duncow," "Tibby Hyslop's Dream" and "The Cameronian Preacher's Tale."

All of these three tales share a theme of dreadful truth being made known through supernatural agency, yet such is Hogg's variety of idiom that, in a way which is typical of the range of all those mentioned above, they are each told in a totally different manner. "The Barber of Duncow" is one of Hogg's finest extended pieces of Scots, the tale being told by Will Gordon the tinkler's wife Raighel, to their son-in-law Hob, who wonders how "any reasonable being could be so absurd as to entertain a dread of apparitions." The tale that she tells has only one drawback:

> "When anybody hears it, an disna believe it, the murdered woman is sure to come in."
> "What d'ye say?" cried Hob, in manifest alarm, "plague on the auld randys, gie us nae sickan story as that, for I assure you I winna believe it."[23]

Hogg is in his element with such "trick" situations as this. His comic framework, with Hob getting more and more worked up as the dénouement approaches, is balanced perfectly with a superbly told ghost story in the vernacular, about the barber in a town built by Covenanters who "married a Cameronian lass for the sake o' a wheen dirty bawbees, an' then his happy days were done. He wadna pray an' sing psalms wi' her, and she wadna sing an' drink an' haud the gibberidge wi' him. . . ." This unnatural union ends in murder, with a fine ghost, "something like a human shape, made o' blue light, but it was flickering and unsteady, like a reflection frae something else." Hogg has no superiors at finding the poetic and eerie image for his unearthly scenes, and rarely repeats his imagery.

Cleverly he fuses his two themes here. On the one hand he has Hob to convince in "real" life, and *within* the story he has to convince those who won't believe that a ghost has condemned the barber of murder. With real skill Hogg times the dénouement to suit both parties, with the ending being appropriately and effectively— "Hush! what's that at the door?—"

"Tibby Hyslop's Dream" dispenses with humour, and tells its tale in the "hard-dry, view-it-all-round way of dealing with horror which is quite unique" that the first modern editor of *The Justified Sinner,* Earle Welby, found so striking in that novel. Plainly, and all the more effectively for that, it tells of simple Tibby, not too gifted with brains, but lovely, who is first taken up with apparent kindness by her master Forret, but then realises that he "has borne the brunt of incensed kirk sessions before then"—he is a hypocrite and villain who is a cheater of the widow and fatherless, and tries to have his way with Tibby. Tibby, for all she is a simpleton, delivers a warning then to him which should have told him that this had become a test case. "Never in his life did he bear such a rebuke as he did that day from the tongue of one he had always viewed as a mere simpleton . . . it was a warning of the most sublime and terrible description. . . ."

This sets the scene. As with Robert Wringhim, the sinner has further to go before judgement emerges fully. But with a real and traditional respect for the folk-unity of the tale, Hogg does not forget Tibby, for she is to be involved in his downfall in two ways. First, she has her striking dream:

Tibby Hyslop dreamed, that on a certain spot which she had never seen before between a stone dyke

206

and a . . . woody precipice . . . she saw Mr Forret lying without his hat, with his throat slightly wounded, and blood running from it; but he neither appeared to be dead, not yet dying, but in excellent spirits. He was clothed in a fine new black suit, had full boots on . . . and gilt spurs. A great number of rooks and hooded crows were making free with his person;— some picking out his eyes, some his tongue, and some tearing out his bowels. In place of being distressed by their voracity, he appeared much delighted, . . .[24]

till a raven comes from a black cloud, drives off the rest, and picks out his heart, and he dies. But the story is not merely a vivid dream with a shocking truth to it. The climax of the tale has poetic justice to it, in one of Hogg's finest court-room scenes, when Tibby reluctantly becomes the vital witness in the case which is to determine Forret's success of ruin. With utterly convincing realism Hogg has the case hang on two points; *not* his attempt on her virtue, for Tibby is not one to tell of that, but his attempt to bribe her into giving false witness, which Tibby, with a sincerity and force comparable to Jeannie Deans, will not do, and her simple but obviously reliable memory of the improper cropping of the land under Forret's rule. How can Tibby be sure, ask the lawyers, that pease, corn and aits were grown in the order they were? She remembers, because

There came a great wind ae Sabbath day, in the ninety-sax, and that raised the shearer's wages at Dumfries to three shillings the day. . . . We had a guid deal o' speaking about it, and I said to John Eadie, "What need we grumble? I made sae muckle at shearing the last year, that it's no done yet." And he said, "Ah, Tibby, but wha can hain like you?"[25]

Against this circumstantial detail and utter honesty, Forret's case crumbles. Ironically the person he tried to use twice on account of her simplicity has been the means of his destruction. And more—Timmy realises with horror that the "crowing" lawyers are the agents of destruction of her dream, with the great prosecution lawyer from Edinburgh as the raven. Forret kills himself in just such a place as in her dream shortly after.

Tradition so obviously gives Hogg an almost classic simplicity and unity in these tales, in that he is to an extent merely the medium of their transmission. All the more credit goes to him when he *creates* his idiom and material more fully, as he does in "The Cameronian's Preacher's Tale," told in that sermon and enthusiastic Presbyterian manner of the sinner, Robert Wringhim, but this time from the point of view that Providence is genuinely working out justice after murder through the preacher who tells the tale.

> I have preached and ye have profited; but what I am about to say is far better than man's preaching, it is one of those terrible sermons which God preaches to mankind, of blood unrighteously shed, and most wondrously avenged. . . . His presence is visible in it; and I reveal it that its burden may be removed from my soul, so that I may die in peace."[26]

The tale is familiar, very like that of "The Fords of Callum"; but the sonorous and intense presentation adds a layer much as the sinner's account adds that deeper layer to the Editor's version of the same events in *The Justified Sinner*. It also permits an atmosphere of eerie landscape to be introduced which the comic presentation of "The Barber of Duncow" and the simplicity of "Tibby Hyslop" prevented. The discovery of the murdered man's grave illustrates this exactly.

> All Crake's Moss seemed on fire; not illumined with one steady and uninterrupted light, but kindled up by fits like the northern sky with its wandering streamers. On a little bank which rose in the centre of the morass, the supernatural splendour seemed chiefly to settle; and having continued to shine for several minutes, the whole faded and left but one faint gleam behind. I fell on my knees, held up my hands to heaven, and said, "This is of God; behold in that fearful light the finger of the most high. . . ."[27]

The whole story is lit by this fitful corpse-light; and few writers can evoke its eerie atmosphere like Hogg. Even John Wilson was forced to admit that this was one of Hogg's best tales.

There is one outstanding feature of his finest supernatural tales of the second group, those which use devils, brownies, and other unearthly agents in the manner of *The Justified Sinner*. The three finest of these, which must show Hogg as one of the undisputed masters of the short story form, all use that clever device of the novel, whereby the events are presented with a wonderful and disturbing *ambiguity* which is quite deliberate. There is also exactly the same method of providing language and diabolic metaphors which, unlike *An Edinburgh Bailie,* are not basically redundant and only there for atmosphere, but have a vital part to play in providing and sustaining the ambiguity. Let us look at the three in turn.

"Mary Burnet" tells of a young man's lovelust

for a pure young girl. He, "as the story goes, uttered in his heart an unhallowed wish—he wished that some witch or fairy would influence his Mary. . . . This wish was thrice repeated, with all the energy of disappointed love . . . thrice repeated, and no more, when behold Mary appeared on the brae. . . ." Of all Hogg's tales, this has the strange elementary morality which is almost amorality, and the ancient "rules of the Game" which are the controlling features of the folktale. This Mary, or her likeness, drowns herself rather than submit—but amazingly, when Jock goes to her home to confess that he has been her destroyer, she is still abed. It is concluded that either the mermaid of the loch or a fairy has met Jock—"but whether a guid ane or an ill ane is hard to determine."

Jock has been given a terrible unearthly warning to stop his evil ways. But Mary's parents are troubled by the strange change in her. "What will you say if it should turn out that our daughter *is* drowned, and that yon was the fairy we had in the house a' the night and this morning?" They never find out. Like Kilmeny, Mary vanishes: her seventh hayrick is unfinished, and however hard they search, all that turns up is a rumour from a crazy old woman that she went by in a grand chariot with Jock Allanson.

Bonny Mary Burnet was lost. She left her father's house at nine o'clock on a Wednesday morning, the seventeenth of September, neatly dressed in a white jerkin and a green bonnet, with her hay-raik over her shoulder. . . .[28]

This is the "Kilmeny" atmosphere completely, with an addition of obvious fairy clues, like the use of the number seven, the old woman's vision (which no one heeds, since she always speaks in "parables") and the green-and-white which are the colours always worn by the fairies. Hay raiks too seem to have an association with unearthly powers—one recalls the last glimpses of Robert Wringhim with his enchanted hay-ropes in which he hanged himself. There is even a Ballad lament for her going inserted here, in the "Kilmeny" manner.

Strangest of all is the fact that Jock Allanson is found at the time of her disappearance to have been raving in a fever of "witches, spirits, and Mary Burnet." This is the first inexplicable part of the tale, with the parents' lament linking it with the even stranger sequel, where Allanson, unreformed, grows "ten times more wicked than before" and is feared as "the Wicked One." The judgement upon him follows apace. Jock goes to the October Hiring fair for no good purpose, the haunt of men who are after the fresh country girls looking for service. He is then drawn to a beautiful green and white clad maiden who seems also to seek him out, who ultimately tells him she is Mary Burnet. Seven times this happens, with his friends chaffing him and saying that he seems to be "bewitched" by the maiden. Everywhere he goes thereafter she follows him, arousing both guilt and love, horror and desire, and growing more gorgeous all the time. He convinces himself—as Robert Wringhim did to his cost—that she is not of the "other world," but a famous beauty who has singled him out. Such pride must be punished, we know. When he vanishes, having told his friends that he is going to her residence, they go seeking him at the "splendid mansion . . . which glowed with lights as innumerable as the stars of the firmament" where they left him the night before. They had seen him received in at the gate—so imagine their horror and wonder on finding, instead of palace or splendid gateway, neither palace nor gate there, but a tremendous gulf, fifty fathoms deep, and a dark stream foaming below. . . . They went forward to the verge . . . to the very spot on which he saw the gate opened, and there they found marks where a horse had been plunging. Its feet had been over the brink, but it seemed to have recovered itself, and deep, deep down, and far within, lay the mangled corpse of Jock Allanson.[29]

There is a sequel. Seven years after her disappearance, as in "Kilmeny," the parents are still remembering and looking. A little wee man, shrivelled, with "a face scarcely like that of a human creature" (like the Brownie of the Black Haggs), accosts them, asking if they would like to see their daughter again. He tells them she is living and well, and that they will see her "precisely when the shadow of the Holy Cross falls due East" in Moffat. They go, and find a beggar woman with two children who is Mary, happy with her children. After their happy reunion she goes off, never to be seen again, in a glorious gilded chariot with men clad in green-and-gold livery.

I have told the story at length because it is, outside *The Three Perils of Man* and *The Justified Sinner,* and along with "The Brownie of the Black Haggs," his finest evocation of a world which, like that of "Kilmeny," moves strangely between Christian and pagan meaning, combining both to gain the maximum amount of poetic, eerie, and timeless suggestion of wonderful possibilities. But notice one crucial improvement on even the two novels. Instead of being on the one hand straightforward diablerie or having on the other a clean division of interpretation between the supernatural and the rational, these later stories—admittedly only three or four in number—move beyond this to the confident and mature storyteller's position of leaving the possibilities open, in a way that is so typical of the work of that *doyen* of modern and disturbing fantasy, Robert Aikmann. Hogg combines a deliberate awareness of aesthetic suggestion, without imposing interpretations, with traditional material. He does not intrude, but allows the last word to the wondering participants in the story:

He only, who made the spirits of men, . . . and all the spirits that sojourn in the earth and the air, can tell how this is. We are wandering in a world of enchantment, and have been influenced by some agencies above human nature or without its pale. . . . How can human comprehension make anything of this?"[30]

Strictly speaking these tales go beyond ambiguity to wonder. "The Brownie of the Black Haggs" is as fine a tale, with its inscrutable, mysterious and ageless visitant who comes as judgement on the wicked Lady Wheelhope, acting within the story as a catalyst which draws the poison latent in each protagonist much as Heathcliff draws the latent self-destroying tendencies out of all who abuse him in *Wuthering Heights.* Indeed, "The Brownie of the Black Haggs" has much to offer the reader of Emily Brönte's novel, since in essence it contains the same situation. An evil family offends Divine Justice, which sends its agent to eradicate the evil. There is an even greater tautness and unity of shape in this short story, but since it is available in *Scottish Short Stories 1800-1900* with commentary,[31] I pass to "Mr Adamson of Laverhope," where, as with "The Brownie of the Black Haggs," a miniature version of *The Justified Sinner* enacts itself. Like Lady Wheel-hope, Mr Adamson incurs heaven's wrath with his ungovernable temper, which causes him to "act the part of a devil" towards fatherless children and their mother, which, as we know, is always attended by Providential appearances of the Devil. The agent is an old gaberlunzie, Patie Maxwell, used to working at odd jobs for Adamson, but on this occasion shamefully mistreated by him. It is certainly Maxwell himself who first appears, and is abused by Adamson. But, after Patie's curse, who is it that appears in his monstrous likeness when that terrible black cloud comes from a clear sky and causes the unnatural storm which totally destroys Adamson's flock and finishes him off in the shocking lightning flash? The old gaberlunzie vows that he was forty miles off that day, and tradition has it that it was "the devil, waiting for his prey, and that he fled away in that sheet of flame carrying the soul of John Maxwell with him."

The other stories of this rich supernatural vein are full of life and flashes of humour, with a wealth of material that should fascinate the folk-lorist as well as entertain the lay reader; but they make use of a more straightforward diablerie. "The Mysterious Bride" tells of a laird's expiation of his father's sins, when the jilted bride-to-be of the father comes back to tryst with the son; "The Laird of Cassway" has a witch prevent a duel between two sons by causing the father to present himself between them—even though he was many miles away at the time; "The Witches of Traquair," "A Story of the Black Arts" and "Grizel Grahame" tell rumbustious and extravagant tales of enchantment and *diablerie* in the manner of the Auchtermuchty story from *The Justified Sinner,* and *The Three Perils of Man.*

What does emerge from a reading of these colourful, fast-moving tales which are so much more authentic and traditional than the material of contemporary and later fantasy writers from Hoffmann and MacDonald to Lewis and Tolkien, is simply how self-impoverishing Hogg's contemporaries were being in excluding this kind of imaginative luxury. There is also the deeper tragedy that Hogg now only occasionally allowed his folk-imagination to take full rein, and even then for a short gallop only. Never again was he to risk an extended Border Romance, or a long fabulous tale.

Looking around the remainder of his stories, one finds that the closer the connection is with his Border material, the better the story. A staple of these later years was the straightforward "Long Pack" type of story which he could write with ease, and for which there was a growing market from about 1829 on in the Annuals and Anniversary volumes. "The Laidlaws and the Scotts," "A Story of Good Queen Bess," and the later stories written to fill the *Tales of the Wars of Montrose,* "Mary Montgomery" and "Wat Pringle of the Yair," are competent tales of missing heirs, mysterious plots, and dramatic scenes of action, with glimpses of the younger Hogg's interests in morbid psychology and ironic anti-romance. This staple material may be set in a Highland background, since Hogg had been familiar with the north and west from his work on *Jacobite Relics*. With this change, but comparable to the Border versions, are "Julia MacKenzie," and "Ewan MacGhabhar," the best of this kind.

But there is no doubt that for all the attempts to develop a new area of imaginative release and for all that Hogg could still write superb supernatural stories and good mysteries, he had lost interest in undertaking any really ambitious project. For most of the years 1825-30, and quite blatantly from 1830 till he died, he was content to fall back on sketches of country courtship done in a chapbook manner, like "Widow Wat's Courtship" or "Katie Cheyne," or to write rather conventional moralistic stories like "Sound Morality," "The Prodigal Son," "Mary Melrose," "The Minister's Annie," "A Border Beauty," and "Nancy Chisholm." Often there is indeed a spark of fire in these, as in the intensity of situation which leads up to the moral denouement in "Aunt Susan" or "Rob Dodds"—but, as we shall shortly see, Hogg was increasingly giving in to pressure to write material either of the "Border life and work" kind, or tending towards the kailyard. Both of these were sad developments for a man who was still in his prime, both physically (he was still winning prizes at Border Games) and mentally, as the ocasional lively story shows. Looking at the enormous output of some 80-odd stories, many of them long-short stories and novelettes, together with poetry and biography and other prose works, one is struck by the peculiar nature of Hogg's tragedy. His critics did not "finish him off"; far from it. But they did—and I will attempt to show how—distort his work completely, and succeeded in breaking his own self-confidence in his traditional material, to the point where he reserved his love of the comic, the riotous, the traditional, and the supernatural for his own indulgence. Instead he ground out incongruous "stories of manners," with bizarre Edinburgh drawing room conversations and *Three Perils of Women*-like tasteless clowning because, pathetically, he thought that he was getting closer to the real market.

Alongside these signs of the onset of creative fatigue is the last sad symptom of self-imitation and attempt to recapture the success of yesteryear. "John Paterson's

Mare" was an 1826 attempt[32] to show all those at Blackwood's that he was as clever as ever and as anybody at the old "Chaldee Manuscript" practice of satirical allegory on literary rights of the day. Sadly—in a way that presages the fate of so many of his later short stories—*Blackwood's Magazine* no longer wished to associate itself with lampoons and libels comparable to modern *Private Eye* material, and the milk-and-water imitation of the scurrilous "Chaldee Manuscript" (for Hogg could never bring himself to be really nasty or bitter) went to the *Newcastle Magazine* and obscurity. In 1828-29 Hogg even imitated that series which he loved and hated, the highly successful "Noctes Ambrosianae" of John Wilson in *Blackwood's* which made an image of him famous for drinking and volatility and a naïve gift for purple lyrical poetry. Hogg wrote two "Noctes Bengerianae" for *The Edinburgh Literary Journal.* But a series by the authentic shepherd was obviously not what the world wanted. As always, they wanted an edited and carefully stage-managed version of the Shepherd. Finally, in poetry as well as in fiction, Hogg began to reproduce successful styles of the past—"A Remarkable Egyptian Story," for example, repeats the manner of the Friar's Tale in *The Three Perils of Man,* with its pseudo-Hebraic language and biblical manner of presentation. He even, in these later years, took material out of *The Three Perils of Man* and re-presented it as new. "Marion's Jock" in *Altrive Tales,* 1832, was the Laird of Peatstocknowe's Tale. Indeed, the later and good Border warfare tales like "Mary Montgomery" are direct descendants and imitations of Charlie Scott's Tale.

But if any final proof of Hogg's loss of creative interest is required, one need only scan the material he wrote in the last two years of his life for *Chamber's Literary Journal*. These are tired, short pieces, and in two cases they are direct, and undistinguished, reprints from *The Edinburgh Literary Journal* of 1829.

* * *

This study has deliberately focussed its attention on Hogg's fiction, rather than his poetry, for the two reasons that firstly I maintain that he is to be assessed as a major writer mainly on account of his achievement in the novel and short story; and secondly because I believe that his considerable achievement in poetry has already been sensitively assessed by Simpson and Mack. But no account of the last ten years of Hogg's work would be complete unless it left the reader with an overall impression of the man and the total body of his work. I have separated the discussion of his later fiction from facts of biography and other literary achievement, the more to highlight his development in that most important area. I should like now to quickly retrace the last ten years, looking at them from the broader perspective of all that was happening to and being written by Hogg.

Hogg's poetry has already been dealt with in the second chapter, when much of the later work of importance was discussed as being the natural development from poems like "The Witch of Fife," "Old David" and "Kilmeny." There are three areas of interest that remain.

It will be remembered that after the failure of his dramas and of the long poems *The Pilgrims of the Sun* and *Mador of the Moor,* Hogg had determined that "save now and then, in an idle song to beguile a leisure hour, to write no more poetry."[33] But by 1824 he must have thought twice about this, since his novels were regarded as failures, and his *Eminent Men* were lying still-born on his hands, no publisher willing to take them on. He had started an epic poem many years before, but abandoned it after two books. Now he remembered it, and completed *Queen Hynde,* publishing it in 1825. "It really belongs with the other poems of 1813-1817," says Mack; but it also has its place in this last period of Hogg's development, because it enables us more fully to understand how completely demoralised he must have been when this venture was received with disdain along with the others. Indeed, he must have been especially hurt, since, unlike his amended view of his novels, he continued all his life to assert that it was "infinitely superior" to *The Queen's Wake,* "the best epic poem that had ever been produced in Scotland." Apart from yet again illustrating Hogg's total inability to judge his own work, so thoroughly had he been disorientated by frequent criticism from any real personal and valid critical values, it is to the failure of this poem that we owe much of the later fiction.

Having been so much discouraged by the failure of *Queen Hynde,* I gave up all thought of ever writing another long poem, but continued for six years to write fairy tales, ghost stories, songs and poems for periodicals. . . .[34]

I do not agree with Douglas Mack that the poem is a complete failure. True, it is a long-drawn, rambling tale of Scotland in "that mythic period" when "facts may be invented at pleasure," and the result is a jumble of Norse berserkers, Celtic Christian priests, chivalrous knights, and very anachronistic, emancipated and wilful ladies. True, the verse gallops along in couplets in a doggerel fashion without any variation,

219

and there is no evidence of reflection above the level of the conventional and mundane. It is no *Don Juan*, after which it is clearly modelled, since there is little depth to the character and less wit. But oddly enough, it entertains and is easy to read, probably because the plot is so simple to follow, though complex, and there is real evidence of Hogg's fantastic imagination underneath, in his creation of an ancient and many-towered Scottish capital, in its bold outline of Norse villains and an Irish-Scottish hero decidedly like Havelok, its scheming minx, "the wicked Wene," who baits surly abbots and steals the hearts of princes. Mainly, though, it reads well for its good humour. It is not meant to be taken seriously. The most serious things in it are the author's remonstrances to his Edinburgh readers which occur at the end of each book, where he gives, without realising it, real clues to his love-hate relationship with his blue-stocking critics.

> Maid of Dunedin, thou may'st see
> Though long I strove to pleasure thee
> That now I've changed my timid tone
> And sing to please myself alone;
> And thou wilt read when well I wot
> I care not whether you do or not. . . .

This would have been an admirable stand at this point in Hogg's career, were it meant; but within a few lines, after saying that he will follow his own impulse, whether it lead him to "the sea-maid's coral dome/or fairy's visionary home . . . or raise up spirits of the hill," he capitulates once again, pleading for understanding on the grounds that his genius is untutored:

> 'Tis Nature's error, so am I.
> Then, oh forgive my wandering theme,

> Pity my faults but do not blame!
> Short my advantage, small my lore . . .
> Then leave to all his fancies wild
> Nature's own rude untutored child. . . .[35]

Apart from our justified scepticism that Nature's child should make its apologia in such conventional terms, the passage illustrates perfectly Hogg's real unsureness of stance and his ominous willingness to take refuge in a position dangerously close to the kailyard. His poetry will increasingly flow from this false source.

This plea turns bitter as the poem goes on, and real disillusion speaks out at the end of Book Five, when he rails against those who "with proud and pompous air/with simpering frown, or nose elate/. . . name the word INDELICATE . . ." admitting that "oft hast thou grieved his heart full sore" especially with the mocking "smile, more cutting far than all;/The praise, half-compliment, half mock,/The minstrel's name itself a joke." This is Hogg's most sustained effusion of hurt, especially when he attacks the "warm friends professed, yet covert foes" who really dislike seeing "a peasant's soul assume its right."[36]

There is in *Queen Hynde* real sign of a poetic talent that could, with genuine discussion and advice, have matured into real comic producing genius, a balance of the epic and humorous which would have been the poetic equivalent of *The Three Perils of Man*. After all, he could sustain marvellously funny parodies of the best poets, so what indeed was lacking, bar the confidence, the maturity, and the poise, to let him develop his own unique voice? Even allowing that Hogg had in *Queen Hynde* cut himself off, on Scott's advice, from the rich source of supernatural incident and "Witch of Fife" comedy, there is real humour, vitality, and freshness of content and tone remaining.

It is principally Hogg's humour which has been under-estimated. In addition to the successful earlier poems discussed, Hogg continued in "Connel of Dee," "The Russiade," "the Powris of Moseke," "The P and the Q," "The Carle of Invertime," "The Miser's Warning" and many others to throw convention to the winds and to parallel his wild imaginings in fiction like "Allan Gordon" with bizarre stories of comic heroes like the incredible Russell. In a tight spot, this Charlie Scott takes on hordes of enemies with his only weapon a table.

> Swords, lances, pitchforks, men and all
> Bore with his table gainst the wall
> Their bodies squeezed as thin as paper,
> And laughed to see them grin and caper;
> While squirting blood so fiercely played
> That holes were in the ceiling made.—
> Now gallant muse, I think thou'll show 'em
> Thou canst indite heroic poem.[37]

Without claiming that this is the finest of verse, it can be argued that Hogg had a real comic bent that in a more robust age would have been encouraged. Significantly, many of these comic epics are simply abandoned, like "The Russiade," or cut off abruptly, with evidence of loss of interest, as with *Queen Hynde*. Many of these comic efforts were collected by Hogg in *A Queer Book* of 1832.

Hogg's songs are also disproportionately successful when they are comic. The earlier collection "The Forest Minstrel" of 1810 is filled with stereotyped post-Burnsian effusions, but significantly leaps in quality in the sections called "Humorous Songs" and "National

Songs." Here the verdict of time has for once been fair, with Mack summing it up admirably.

> Hogg's work as a song-writer has been overshadowed by the pre-eminence of Burns in the same field, but his achievement is nevertheless considerable. In particular, his pastoral songs and many of his love songs are remarkable for the mood of calm and tranquil beauty which they evoke.[38]

When Hogg wrote book songs, he wrote them from a totally different point of view from that of Burns. His love poems too often are synthetic, as though he feels he must celebrate Maggie's (or Jeannie's or Peggy's or Annie's) charms; the public expect this from a peasant poet. It comes as an incongruous but correcting thought after reading these to remember that many of these which were churned out for the periodicals of the 1820s and 1830s were written by a happily married man in his fifties and sixties, with a growing family, who could not possibly have had the time to even begin acquaintance with these assorted ladies.

But I would agree with Mack that in these later years there is the ocasional sober and mature note to be heard in his verse. In poems like "The Monitors," "St Mary of the Lowes," and "Ringan and May" there is a control, a reflective beauty in contrast to the usual work of the riotous poet of "The Witch of Fife," a development from the delicacy of feeling of the earlier "Verses Addressed to . . . Anne Scott of Buccleuch." When Hogg remembers and celebrates his own harmonious domestic and country life and affairs with simple dignity and without conventionality he comes close to being a great poet.

But in his poetry even more than in his fiction he was afflicted by the opinions of his peers. He was never sure as to language, or as to mood. His successes were coincidental, and his totally unified achievements rare. Even his famous "A Boy's Song" comes perilously close to ruining its simplicity and unaffected natural progress with its prim moral, intruded to suit an alien taste.

> Why the boys should drive away
> Little sweet maidens from the play,
> Or love to banter and fight so well,
> That's the thing I never could tell.[39]

Much of his dilemma as a poet is revealed in that verse. But as a final assessment this is ungracious. His faults have been fully analysed by Simpson, especially. The poet whose "Skylark," "Donald MacDonald," "Charlie is my Darling," "When the Kye comes Hame," "Lock the Door Lariston" and many other songs, who came so close to recapturing the true Ballad note in "A Lay of the Martyrs" and "The Liddel Bower," who rescued so many fine Jacobite songs from obscurity, has a certain right to claim

> I'll leave them canty sangs will reach
> From John o' Groats to Solway strand.
> Then what are houses, goud, or land,
> To sic an heirship left in fee?
> An' I think mair o' auld Scotland
> Than to be fear'd for me and mine.[40]

* * *

Let us hope that posterity will continue to justify Hogg's faith. Certainly in his own time, from 1825 on, his critics and peers did him little good, his hopes for a Royal Society of Literature pension (a cause pushed hard by Lockhart) being dashed when William Jerdan told him in 1827 that their help was "for the encouragement of learning rather than of that kind of literature which may be sustained by making itself popular."[41] Hogg was getting more and more desperate now, since not only his literary but his farming efforts were failing, and, although humorously put, he is being nothing but truthful when he tells Blackwood that his wife Margaret

> was just saying she had forgot the time she had money in her pocket. And I replied I had the shilling in my possession which I kept alone since the Border Games.[42]

What Abbotsford was to Walter Scott, Mount Benger was to Hogg. His life had become something of an ironic and vicious circle. Mount Benger needed all the attention that Hogg could give it, and it needed money ploughed into it too. The money could only come from writing, which required time which was needed on the farm. Besides, although Hogg was by now world famous, he could not get his novels published. To further complicate this tortuous situation, there were the visitors, coming all the time, sometimes thirty in a day:

> We had twelve yesterday, and there were five ladies and two gentlemen . . . and their friends did us the pleasure of staying with us six weeks. Really this false and unwanted popularity that comes too late is far too much. It is utter ruination. . . .[43]

All this came to a head in April 1830. Hogg lost both the favour of the Duke of Buccluech from a misunderstanding over alleged poaching on Hogg's part, and two thousand pounds on Mount Benger. A

Warrant of Sale was subscribed against him, and Hogg had to return to his rent-free Altrive, feeling it "rather hard to have to begin the world anew at sixty years of age."

Understandably, he grew more and more anxious about his stories from 1825 on. They became in his eyes the only way of redeeming his desperate financial situation. In 1826 he wanted Blackwood to publish four volumes of *Scottish Tales* and *The Shepherd's Calendar*. By 1830 the project needed twelve volumes, and shortly afterwards he tried frantically to persuade Blackwood that Scott and Lockhart approved of and would help with a twenty-volume collection. By 1833 a twenty-four-volume collection is Hogg's dream. Strout would seem to be right when he claims that Hogg "became the victim of an obsession that he could recoup his losses . . . by inundating an eagerly expectant public with a mass of prose narrative, and that Blackwood and Lockhart would of necessity co-operate with him in his brilliant comeback."[44]

Of course this was just a "saving lie" with which Hogg kept up his self-esteem, sorely tried in these ten years, as Blackwood refused *Eminent Men* and all his ambitious schemes. It is true that Blackwood published *The Shepherd's Calendar* and Hogg's later volumes of poetry, but increasingly he returned Hogg's tales. "An Egyptian Story," "Wat the Prophet," "David Dale," "A Story of the Black Art," "Strange Letter of a Lunatic," "Sandy Elshinder" and "Captain Lochy" were all offered first to Blackwood and then refused.

But of this emerges a point crucial to our understanding of Hogg's relations with the Blackwood Group. He could not rid himself of the conviction that the centre of his literary values and meaningful criticism lay there. The approval of *Blackwood's,* of Wilson and

Lockhart, was as delightful to him as their criticisms were corrosive. It was a love-hate relationship every bit as real and strong as Wringhim's with Gilmartin. First offers of new work, boasts of successes to come, bitterest complaints of hurt and betrayal, are all reserved for that magazine. In the last analysis, *Blackwood's* policy controlled Hogg's career.

Piecing the picture together from the letters and other evidence available, it appears that Hogg had become something of a liability to the group. They talked about him in the terms reserved among close friends for someone *outside* the inner sanctum who thinks that he belongs there. "Don't let Hogg dream I would have anything to do with his edition of novels," says Lockhart to Blackwood in 1831; one can almost see the accompanying raising of shoulders and looking to heaven to express the exasperated boredom that Hogg should be at him *again* for help.[45] Hogg tries so hard to please—but we realise that it is all to late to change the prejudiced opinions the group have of his abilities.

> I should be very sorry to have "The Marvellous Doctor" rejected as I am sure it will offer great amusement to many of your readers and the professor [Wilson] not the least who knows the ground-work of the story. But as I never pretend to depend on my own taste in matters of modern delicacy if you have any suspicions on that head send the manuscript to Robert [his nephew *amanuensis* who deals with necessary "improvements"]—his slight alterations will completely obliterate any appearance of indelicacy. Mr Lockhart has given me the hint over and over again. . . .[46]

Very occasionally his own intuitive taste asserts itself,

as when he asks the Devil to take Blackwood for not getting his *Shepherd's Calendar* out quickly enough. "There is an absolute necessity exclusive of all other concerns for the collecting of these varied pictures and details of pastoral life." But till 1831 Hogg was to accept the distortions of the "Noctes," half admiring Wilson's diabolic cleverness, half-angry at the very real hurt the false image gave to his wife, who till she died in 1870 never heard the "Noctes" mentioned without flushing with resentment. There seems indeed to have been some clever exploitation of Hogg in these years. One suspects that Blackwood published just enough of Hogg's stuff to keep him uneasily at heel, while his name and pseudo-presence continued to give the life-blood to the series. Wilson and Blackwood needed Hogg's good-will, if they did not want his writing. Wilson in particular (apart from the anonymous abuse of the "Noctes") went some way towards flattering Hogg in these years, as one of Britain's greatest poets, anglers, husbands, masters,—though he qualified this by adding that Hogg was "an indifferent novelist" and "a worse practical farmer." He even admitted that "there is no likeness in James Hogg to the Ettrick Shepherd in the "Noctes Ambrosianae.""

Blackwood's did not play fair with Hogg. It used his name but did not pay him for it; kept his stories for far too long, building up his hopes that something would come of his ambitious scheme for a collection of *Scottish Tales*. Blackwood knew of Hogg's desperate poverty, and Hogg's complaint of 1832 is a typical one, with the ring of truth about it.

It was not because you did not publish Col. Aston that I was offended but because you *promised* to do so and did not; and though you knew I was depending on you solely for a little monthly supply

228

you kept all my best things lying by you from month to month.[47]

In December 1831 Hogg blew up at Wilson's treatment of him in the "Noctes." "Let the proud old aristocrat know that the shepherd despises him as much as the dirt among his feet." He demanded his material back, forbade all use of his name in the series, and virtually disappeared from the magazine from then on. "Maga will be much more uniform without my motley productions which nobody reads and after this you will please mention THE SHEPHERD no more."[48]

But he was so linked in the public mind with the magazine that he became "exceedingly awkwardly placed," since apart from *Fraser's* and the Annuals nobody bothered to ask him to write. He had lost Lockhart's support completely in 1834 with his *Domestic Manners of Sir Walter Scott* and its questioning of Scott's wife's legitimacy of birth, and its picture of Scott as something of a snob (a book now regarded as shedding fresh and important light on Scott from an unusual angle, but not as offensive). His *Altrive Tales* project had fallen through with the collapse of his publisher. All that was keeping him going was the work for the Annuals and his poetry— which Blackwood was canny enough to continue to publish in the volume of *Songs, by the Ettrick Shepherd* of 1831 and *A Queer Book* of 1832. Almost all his other works were out of print.

Wilson was feeling the lack of Hogg's presence from his "Noctes," however, which probably explains his "making-up" of the quarrel between Blackwood and Hogg in 1834. And in Wilson's "terms" for Hogg's return to the magazine in April 1834 the entire Blackwood view of Hogg becomes clear. Hogg was to get fifty pounds per annum for letting the series use his name and image, and

> if you will, instead of writing long tales, for which at present there is no room, write a "Series of Letters to Christopher North," or "Flowers and Weeds from the forest," or "My Life at Altrive," embodying your thoughts and sentiments on all things, ANGLING, shooting, curling, etc., etc., in an easy and characteristic style it will be easy for you to add £50 per annum to the £50 you will receive for your "Noctes."[49]

Thus was Hogg "bought off" and brought back to the fold; thus the transformation of James Hogg, author of *The Three Perils of Man, The Justified Sinner, The Queen's Wake* and *The Poetic Mirror*, to Blackwood's tame Shepherd in Ettrick was completed.

As a final illustration of the view of Hogg's talents that now prevailed I find Archibald Fullerton's request to Hogg of May 1834 one of the most pointed and amusing. He asks for something of "the moral and the humorous" to preface his edition of Burns:

> Do furnish us with something of this kind for the edition.—and something pathetic and tender to the memory of his now departed Bonny Jean! STOP.— A thought just strikes me—I think I see Robin LEANING OVER THE BREAST OF A CLOUD, watching the angels conveying his Jean to heaven! Think of his feelings, and his soliloquy as he eyes their approach! —the manner and circumstances of THEIR MEETING! —and what they would RESPECTIVELY SAY TO EACH OTHER when they had got TIME AND COMPOSURE TO SPEAK.—What an admirable subject for the feeling heart, and splendid imagination, of the Ettrick Shepherd! [50]

Under Wilson's literary monarchy, such kailyard attitudes to Hogg and indeed all Scottish life and literature were to flourish.

In practice *Blackwood's* wanted little from Hogg of his own, and he felt the humiliation, as he tells Blackwood in November 1834.

> Though I cannot but admire the generosity and kindness of the bequest I would much rather it had been for contributions of my own. There is no doubt that North's [Wilson's] Shepherd is a much nobler animal than the Shepherd himself, but the plan is rather too humiliating. I am exactly like an actor who is engaged at a certain salary and yet performs by a substitute claiming a half of the real actor's profits.[51]

Tales of the Wars of Montrose sold only three hundred copies, and was abused in *The Atheneum* and *The Times.* Hogg was reduced to writing *Lay Sermons on Good Principles and Good Breeding* and planning *The Young Lady's Sabbath Companion.* The Spirit of the Age had finally beaten him, and there is a tired resignation—and, for the first time, an expression of age and weariness—in his last letter to all those at *Blackwood's,* August 1835.

> Dear Callants
>   Though I am now excluded from the pages of Maga perhaps I may get a corner by and by.[52]

*　　*　　*

All this paints too gloomy a picture of Hogg's last years. It must be remembered that the connection with Edinburgh was only a part of his life, and that since 1815 he had a secure base in the Borders in Altrive, and from 1820 the happiest of marriages.

One may think, on reading over this memoir, that I must have worn out a life of misery and wretchedness; but the case has been quite the reverse. I never knew either man or woman who has been so uniformly; . . . Indeed, so uniformly smooth and happy has my married life been, that on a retrospect I cannot distinguish one part from another, save by some remarkably good days of fishing, shooting, and curling on the ice.[53]

At fifty-eight he was still winning prizes in the field events at the St Ronan's Games, in Innerleithen, much to the chagrin of younger competitors, and was Captain of the Bowmen of the Border; and at sixty-two he won the Bowman's competition and sweepstake at the same games. Some of his work like the poems and sermons sold well, and he had good and loyal friends in London like Pringle and Alan Cunningham who gave him opportunities to write in the Annuals, and helped arrange his triumphant visit to London in 1832. He was a poor man, and the purpose of his visit, to try to arrange once more for the publication of the collection of his *Scottish Tales,* was doomed to fail. But he was famous, and a host of literary and social lights turned up to the Burns supper at the Free Mason's Hall at which he was the guest of honour. The festivity here and later is well recorded; but in many ways what we find more significant now are two comments. The first is from William Howlett.

Such was my own opinion, derived from this source [the "Noctes"] of Hogg . . . with open mouth and huge straggling teeth, in full roars of drunken laughter, that, on meeting him in London, I was quite amazed to find him so smooth, well-looking, and gentlemanly.[54]

The second is a swift assessment, but penetrating and important, by Thomas Carlyle.

> I do not well understand the man; his significance
> is perhaps considerable. His poetic talent is
> authentic, yet his intellect seems of the weakest; his
> morality limits itself to the precept "be not angry."
> Is the charm of this poor man chiefly to be found
> herein that he *is* a real product of nature, and able
> to speak naturally? . . . The man is a very curious
> SPECIMEN. Alas, he is a MAN; yet how few will so
> much as treat him like a SPECIMEN, and not like a
> mere PUNCH or JUDY.[55]

Hogg died in November 1835. He was buried in Ettrick
Churchyard, beside his grandfather, Will o' Phaup,
who had been the last man to hold converse with the
fairies, and close to where he was born. But even in
his death the relationship with Wilson was to have a
sting in its tail.

Wilson had always acted the part of Hogg's closest
friend, despite the lack of concrete evidence to support
the claim. Now, at the graveside, conscious of the
drama of the situation, he was impressive.

> Who that was present could forget the noble form of
> John Wilson—a model for a sculptor—as he stood
> at the top of the grave, his cloak wrapped round him,
> his head uncovered, his long auburn hair streaming
> in the wind, while tears flowed down his manly
> countenance?[56]

Hogg's widow and family now needed help. Wilson,
as "closest friend," got all the materials from her to
write the biography of Hogg that was necessary to
ensure his fame and the good sale of his works, shortly

to appear in collected form. A subscription raised by a William Scott and Wilson quickly drew in £1400.

But the promised biography was never written, and one discovers that the subscription was "aided by Professor Wilson's name"—no great effort! Alan Cunningham desperately wanted to write the biography of his friend and fellow poet, but had to defer to Wilson's claim. When nothing transpired of the biography, he wrote in March 1836 to Hogg's wife, to find that "all the documents put at the disposal of Wilson were lost or mislaid." He then wrote directly to Wilson. He told Mrs Hogg shortly after that

> To this it has not been the Professor's pleasure to return an answer. . . . But the will of John Wilson be done; he seems above the usual forms of courtesy.[57]

Hogg's wife put up an unpretentious stone; twenty-five years later "some sympathetic souls" raised the present memorial. Eighteen years after Hogg's death his widow, after her heaviest struggles were over and her family grown up, was given a Royal pension of £50. But John Wilson, the self-asserted closest friend of Hogg, neither wrote the biography, nor assisted through the pages of *Blackwood's*, throughout these difficult years—but prevented others from doing what he had promised to do.

But time has its revenges. Who now reads Wilson, or Lockhart (apart from his *Life of Scott*)? *Blackwood's Magazine* might have elevated itself above the fantastic writings of James Hogg, but in the long run its "improvement" in taste led to its loss of colour and vitality.

Hogg was a naive man, as Carlyle saw. He was a shallow political thinker, totally dedicated to his king and country, and prejudiced like Scott against all radical thought, whether in politics or agriculture. He rarely used his intellect with any profundity, although when he did, as in *The Justified Sinner,* he reveals a keen brain, with an instinctive sense of irony and egalitarian charity. What shines out still is the quality of his fantastic imagination and his reductive humour. What his 1865 editor, Thomas Thomson, said of *The Mountain Bard* may be taken as a final tribute to his fiction as well as his poetry.

It is a collection of poetical tales written by an untaught man, who had neither a system to illustrate nor a theory to establish. They are the legends of his own district, handed down through generations of the peasantry through time immemorial, but kindled into life and clothed with beauty by the magic power of his genius, until they rise from mere village tales into something of epic importance and grandeur, as well as life-like reality.

NOTES

1. Quoted in John Carey's edition of *The Justified Sinner,* 1969, p. 256.
2. *New Monthly,* November 1824, p. 506.
3. Alan L. Strout, *The Life and Letters of James Hogg, The Ettrick Shepherd,* Vol. II (1826-1835), unpublished, in typescript in the National Library of Scotland. Hereafter Strout, vol. II. (M.S. 10495).
4. The *Autobiography,* p. 459, says that "in the same year [as *The Justified Sinner*] I offered them [Longman's] "The Lives of Eminent Men" . . . they begged leave to decline." Hogg refers to the collection again in a letter to Blackwood of February 1828, and much more fully, giving contents, in a letter to Blackwood of February 1829,

lamenting the failure to publish these. He had described the contents in exactly the same way to Cunningham in a letter of October 1828;

> I have a MS work by me these several years which Blackwood objected to. . . . I know and am sure it will sell . . . it should come out ere B was aware." [In it are] "Singular Passages in the lives of Eminent Men. . . . These are An Edinr Bailie, Col. Peter Aston, Sir Simon Brodie, Col. Cloud and Mr Alexander McCorkindale. They are all fabulous stories founded on historical facts and would make two small volumes.

There is no "Mr McCorkindale" in Hogg. He amended the name to "Kendale," the hero of "The Baron St Gio." "Allan Gordon," a separate work, is first mentioned to Blackwood in December 1827 as "Polar Curiosities," and was turned down by Blackwood then, and in 1828 by Cunningham. "John Lochy" had been objected to by Blackwood before June 1830, but Hogg obviously worked over this for several years. It is probably the "singular tale in hand" of August 1829. All these letters are quoted in *Strout*, vol. II, pp. 9-21.

5. *Simpson*, p. 205.

6. See list of Hogg's works at end.

7. *Autobiography*, p. 458.

8. *Autobiography*, p. 459.

9. See Chapter 5.

10. *Tales*, vol. I, p. 451.

11. *Tales*, vol. I, p. 430.

12. *Tales*, vol. I, p. 445.

13. *Tales*, vol. I, p. 447.

14. *Tales*, vol. I, p. 473.

15. *Tales*, vol. II, p. 300.

16. *Altrive Tales*, p. 107.

17. *Autobiography*, pp. 456-7.

18. "Some Passages in the Life of Colonel Cloud," *Blackwood's Magazine*, July 1825, p. 40.

19. "Colonel Cloud," p. 40.

20. *Tales and Sketches, by the Ettrick Shepherd*, 1837, vol. I, p. 268.

21. *Tales and Sketches*, vol. I, p. 287.

22. "Balaam" is the reservoir of "filling" material kept by newspapers for lean news-days. Accounts of "enormous turnips grown within a gentleman's garden in Surrey . . ." "new mermaid . . . in Orkney." See Hogg's funny account in "Letters from James Hogg to his Reviewer," *Blackwood's Magazine*, October 1820, p. 69.

23. "The Barber of Duncow," *Fraser's Magazine*, March 1831, p. 174.

24. *Tales,* vol. II, p. 155-156.

25. *Tales,* vol. II, p. 160.   28. *Tales,* vol. II, p. 166.

26. *Tales,* vol. I, p. 300.   29. *Tales,* vol. II, p. 171.

27. *Tales,* vol. I, p. 307.   30. *Tales,* vol. II, p. 171.

31. *Scottish Short Stories 1800-1900,* ed. Douglas Gifford, 1971, introduction and pp. 46-62.

32. The piece was written much earlier, as we know from letters of July 1818 to Blackwood. Hogg was annoyed at "the two devils," Wilson and Lockhart, for his being "banished their too much loved society." "I have been quizzed too much by you chaps already," "Wilson will not let in anything of mine," so rather pathetically he boasts of how this new allegory will out-Chaldee all of *their* stuff (*Strout,* vol. I, pp. 154-156). The fact that Hogg kept trying for eight years to find a place for the piece shows how desperately he wanted to impress "the two devils." See also A. L. Strout, "James Hogg's Forgotten Satire," *Proceedings of the Modern Language Association,* vol. LII, June 1937, pp. 427-460.

33. *Autobiography,* p. 454.   38. *Mack,* p. xv.

34. *Autobiography,* p. 460.   39. *Works,* vol. II, p. 436.

35. *Works,* vol. II, p. 195.   40. *Works,* vol. II, p. 399.

36. *Works,* vol. II, p. 248.   41. *Strout,* vol. II, p. 6.

37. *Works,* vol. 11, p. 298.   42. *Strout,* vol. II, p. 5.

43. *Strout,* vol. II, pp. 86-87.

44. *Strout,* vol. II, p. 36.   49. *Strout,* vol. II, p. 90.

45. *Strout,* vol. II, p. 53.   50. *Strout,* vol. II, p. 91.

46. *Strout,* vol. II, p. 10.   51. *Strout,* vol. II, p. 100.

47. *Strout,* vol. II, p. 66.   52. *Strout,* vol. II, p. 105.

48. *Strout,* vol. II, p. 54.   53. *Autobiography,* p. 459.

54. William Howlett, *Homes and Haunts of the Most Eminent British Poets,* 1847, vol. II, p. 37.

55. Thomas Carlyle, "Extracts from Notebooks," in J. A. Froude, *Thomas Carlyle: A History of the First Forty Years of his Life, 1798-1835,* 1882, vol. II, quoted *Strout,* vol. II, p. 58.

56. James Russell, *Reminiscences of Yarrow,* pp. 193-195.

57. *Strout,* vol. II, p. 108.

58. *Works,* vol. II, p. 61.

A CHRONOLOGICAL LIST OF HOGG'S WRITING

In the list below, I have gone into greatest detail in respect of the fiction, since information on the poetry can be found in the bibliography of *Batho*. All short stories, unless otherwise indicated, were published in *Blackwood's Magazine*. "S.M.' refers to *The Scots Magazine;* "E.L.J." to the *Edinburgh Literary Journal;* "F.M." to *Fraser's Magazine;* and "C.L.J." to *Chambers's Literary Journal*. "N.F." means non-fiction, * *Shepherd's Calendar*. Major works, like separate volumes and novels, are italicised; short stories, sketches and poems are in quotation marks. The aim of the guide is not only to give dates of publication; where necessary it records discrepancies between time of composition and publication.

1801	*Scottish Pastorals, Poems, Songs, Etc.*
1802/3	"A Journey Through the Highlands of Scotland" (SM).
1805/6	"Journal of an Excursion into the Counties of Stirling, Perth and Kinross" (SM).
1807	*The Mountain Bard; The Shepherd's Guide* (Treatise on Diseases of Sheep).
1808/9	"A Journey Through the Highlands and Western Isles" (SM).
1810	*The Forest Minstrel*; *The Spy* (Periodical which ran for a year) *cf.* note 1, pp. 98-99; and note 25, p. 100.
1812	"Rose Selby" (SM).
1813	*The Queen's Wake; The Hunting of Badlewe.*
1814	*Mador of the Moor; The Pilgrims of the Sun; The Poetic Mirror.*
1815	*Hebrew Melodies; Dramatic Tales.*
1817	"The Long Pack" (published individually); "A Country Wedding"; "The Chaldee Manuscript" (NF).
1818	*The Brownie of Bodsbeck; The Hunt of Eildon* (and "The Woolgatherer," from *The Spy*); *"The Shepherd's Dog" (NF).
1819	"Storms" (NF); *The Jacobite Relics of Scotland* (first series).
1820	*Winter Evening Tales* contained the stories marked (S) in *The Spy* list, plus *The Bridal of Polmood*, "An Old Soldier's Tale," "Cousin Mattie," "Welldean Hall," "Tibby Johnstone's Wraith," "John Gray o' Middleholme"; ("Highland Adventures" (NF) is from "Malise's Tour in the Highlands" in *The Spy*); four Letters (NF). *Cf.* note 1, pp. 98-99.

1821	*The Jacobite Relics of Scotland* (second series).
1822	*The Three Perils of Man; The Poetical Works of James Hogg; The Royal Jubilee.*
1823	*The Three Perils of Women* (three stories); *"Robb Dodds"; *"Mr Adamson of Laverhope."
1824	*The Justified Sinner;* *Lasses"; "Captain Napier" (NF).
1825	"Colonel Cloud"; *Queen Hynde;* (it is also probable that *The Edinburgh Bailie,* "Peter Aston," "Simon Brodie" and "The Baron St. Gio" which Hogg intended to make up two volumes called *Lives of Eminent Men,* were written about this time, although not published until later;—*see* chapter VI).
1826	"John Paterson's Mare" (*Newcastle Magazine*).
1827	*"Sheep," *"Prayers," *"Odd Characters" (all NF); *"George Dobson's Expedition to Hell"; *"The Souters of Selkirk"; *"Tibby Hyslop's Dream"; *"The Laird of Winsholm"; *"The Laird of Cassway"; *"The Marvellous Doctor"; (It is also probable that "Polar curiosities," mentioned by Hogg to Blackwood at this time, is in fact "The Surpassing Adventures of Allan Gordon"; *see* chapter VI).
1828	*"Trials of Temper"; *Mary Burnet"; *"The Witches of Traquair"; *"A Strange Secret"; *"The Brownie of the Black Haggs"; "A Letter from Yarrow" (NF) (ELJ), "Noctes Bengerianae I" (ELJ); ("The Adventures of Captain John Lochy" was certainly begun by this time, though it seems to have developed till 1832).
1829	*The Shepherd's Calendar* included all the above marked * plus "Nancy Chisholm" and "The Prodigal Son." "The Wanderer's Tale" (ELJ); "Sound Morality"; "A Tale of the Martyrs"; "A Letter about Men and Women"; "Wat the Prophet" (ELJ); "Anecdotes of Highlanders" (ELJ); "The Pongos"; "A Story of the '46" (ELJ); "The Cameronian Preacher's Tale" (in *The Anniversary*). *Cf.* note 1, pp. 98-99.
1830	"Dr David Dale's Account of a Grand Aerial Voyage" (ELJ) (mentioned *Strout* 1828); "A Letter from Yarrow" (ELJ) (NF); "The Baron St. Gio"; "Adam Scott"; "The Unearthly Witness" (FM); "Julia Mackenzie"; "Sandy Elshinder" (ELJ); "The Mysterious Bride"; "The Fords of Callum"; "The Strange Letter of a Lunatic" (FM) (mentioned *Strout* 1828).
1831	"A Story of the Black Arts" (ELJ) (mentioned *Strout* 1828); "The Laidlaws and the Scotts" and "The Bogle of the Brae" (in Picken's *The Club Book*); "The

Barber of Duncow" (FM); "The Minister's Annie" (ELJ); "A Tale of Good Queen Bess"; "Aunt Susan" (FM); "An Awfu' Leein'-Like Story"; "On the Separate Existence of the Soul" (FM); "Grizel Graham" (ELJ); "Epitaph on Two Living Characters" (FM); *Songs by the Ettrick Shepherd*.

1832   *Altrive Tales* contained "John Lochy" (mentioned *Strout* 1828); "Marion's Jock" reprinted from *The Three Perils of Man*, and "The Pongos" reprinted from *Blackwood's* 1829; "Ewan McGabhar"; "A Tale of an Old Highlander" *(Metropolitan)*; "Some Terrible Letters from Scotland" *(Metropolitan)*; *A Queer Book*.

1833   "A Remarkable Egyptian Story"; "Emigration" (CLJ); "The Watchmaker" (CLJ); "An Old Minister's Tale" (CLJ); "An Adventure of the Ettrick Shepherd" (CLJ); "A Letter from Canada" (CLJ).

1834   "The Extraordinary History of a Border Beauty" (FM); "The Frasers in the Correi" (FM); ("A Story of the '46" and "Anecdotes of the Highlanders" were reprinted from ELJ in CLJ); *The Domestic Manners and Private Life of Sir Walter Scott; Lay Sermons*.

1835   *Tales of the Wars of Montrose* contained *An Edinburgh Bailie*, "Peter Aston," "Simon Brodie" (all mentioned *Strout* 1828), "Julia Mackenzie" (reprinted from *Blackwood's* 1830), "Watt Pringle o' the Yair," "Mary Montgomery"; "Anecdotes of Ghosts" (FM).

1836   "The Turners" (FM); "Helen Crocket" (FM).

1837†   *Tales and Sketches by the Ettrick Shepherd* contained in six volumes the works of which Hogg himself approved, with revisions carried out shortly before his death and, not before printed, "Alan Gordon," "A Tale of Pentland," "Katie Cheyne," "Nature's Magic Lantern" and "Gordon the Gypsy." The versions of *The Justified Sinner* and *The Three Perils of Man* are drastically altered to *The Confessions of a Fanatic* and *The Siege of Roxburgh* respectively.

1838/40 *The Poetical Works of the Ettrick Shepherd*.

1865   *The Works of the Ettrick Shepherd*, ed. T. Thomson.

1886   *The Tales of James Hogg, the Ettrick Shepherd*.

† This collection omitted *The Three Perils of Women*. Most of the non-fiction listed above was not reprinted; neither were most of the short stories which were not published by Blackwood's.